mini Dubai

The Essential **Visitors'** Guide

Dubai mini Explorer 1st Edition
ISBN 10 976-8182-40-7
ISBN 13 978-976-8182-40-7

Copyright © Explorer Group Ltd 2006
All rights reserved.

All maps © Explorer Group Ltd 2006

Front cover photograph – Victor Romero
Special thanks to photographer Ahmed Alshehi

Printed and bound by
Emirates Printing Press, Dubai, UAE

Explorer Publishing & Distribution
PO Box 34275, Zomorrodah Building,
Za'abeel Rd, Dubai , United Arab Emirates
Phone (+971 4) 335 3520 **Fax** (+971 4) 335 3529
Email Info@Explorer-Publishing.com
Web www.Explorer-Publishing.com

While every effort and care has been made to ensure the accuracy of the information contained in this publication, the publisher cannot accept responsibility for any errors or omissions it may contain.

No part of this publication may be reproduced, stored in a retrieval system, or transmitted, in any form or by any means, electronic, mechanical, photocopying, recording or otherwise, without the prior permission in writing of the publisher.

Introduction

It could be the man-made islands the size of Manhattan or the ski slope in the desert, but Dubai has gained a certain reputation for the sublime and the outrageous. You'll find both, and everything in between, in the pages of this 1st Edition of *Dubai mini Explorer*. The team behind the bestselling residents' guide, *Dubai Explorer*, have dipped into more than a decade of hard-earned knowledge to bring you Dubai's best bits. Happy exploring.

The Explorer Team

Looking for an easier and more enjoyable property experience?

Leading the way in Dubai real estate for over 20 years, Better Homes has the finest and most comprehensive listings of property in the region; selling, leasing and managing more properties than any other agency in the Gulf.

So whether you want to buy, sell, rent or lease, need a place to live or a place to work – look no further.

With helpful, trustworthy advice from the only trained and certified property consultants in the UAE, we take the 'pain' out of property and make the whole process as smooth as possible.

Based in the UAE we have offices located throughout Dubai and Sharjah whilst internationally we are now opening offices across the Middle East, Asia, Europe and North America. In fact, all over the world people are discovering an easier and more enjoyable property experience.

"Better call **Better Homes**"

Sales
Leasing
Short-term Rentals
Property Management
Commercial Advisory
Project Sales & Marketing
Engineering
Interiors.

+971 4 344 7714 enquiries@bhomes.com www.bhomes.com

betterhomes

...because no one understands property better

Contents

Overview

Overview

Prime location

Endless desert gives way to rugged mountains, and skyscrapers shadow windtowers in this contrary corner of the Arabian Gulf.

The United Arab Emirates sits proudly on the north-eastern tip of the Arabian Peninsula, bordered by Saudi Arabia to the south and west and the Sultanate of Oman to the east and north. The country is made up of seven emirates (Abu Dhabi, Ajman, Dubai, Fujairah, Sharjah, Umm Al Quwain, and Ras Al Khaimah. Abu Dhabi, which occupies over 80% of the country, is the biggest emirate, with Dubai the second largest.

In contrast to Dubai's glittering skyline and never-ending construction, the coast of the UAE is littered with coral reefs and over 200 islands, most of which are uninhabited.

The majority of the country is desert, but to the east, rise the impressive Hajar Mountains. Lying close to the Gulf of Oman, they form a backbone through the country, from the Mussandam Peninsula in the north, through the eastern UAE and into Oman.

The Rub Al Khali, more commonly known as the Empty Quarter, occupies a swathe of the south of the country – its desert punctuated by the occasional oasis and spectacular dunes. Common to Saudi Arabia, Oman and Yemen, it is the largest sand desert in the world, covering an area roughly the same size as France, Belgium and the Netherlands.

Despite its ridiculously ambitious architecture and lengthening list of new developments, Dubai is made up largely of arid desert and with sometimes breathtaking sand dunes hiding the odd oasis.

This juxtaposition of geography coupled with incredibly high temperatures limits the variety of flora and fauna present, but you'd be surprised at just how green parts of the UAE are, and Dubai is no exception. It helps that the country's government is spending time and money on its 'greening' programme – don't be surprised to see well-maintained grass, healthy palm trees and pretty flowers lining endless roads. And some mightily impressive golf courses, come to that.

But one issue that the UAE is still struggling to overcome is water consumption – currently the highest per capita in the world. A desalination complex has been built in Jebel Ali in an attempt to combat the lack of ground water and meet this near-impossible demand, but the question of long-term

Way to go

With an ultra-modern international airport, as well as neighbouring Abu Dhabi and Sharjah servicing visitors, Dubai is well equipped for an influx of visitors. And flight times from most major cities are more than reasonable.

From	Flight (in hrs)
Hong Kong	9
Johannesburg	8
London	7
Mumbai	3
New York	14
Osaka	8
Paris	8
Sydney	15

(Source: Emirates Airlines)

sustainability has still not been answered. Despite the harsh environment, indigenous nature and wildlife still thrive, with over 3,500 plants endemic to the country, as well as extensive fauna. Though as you'd expect, the most common animals are camels and goats, who are often seen roaming dangerously close to the roadside. The birdlife here is reasonably extensive too, but it's the coastline, home to an impressive array of natural life, that really takes your breath away. A myriad of tropical fish, as well as a variety of sharks, dolphins and the dugong (sea cow) make up the awesome marine life, which draws divers and snorkellers from all over the world. With various breeds of turtle also indigenous to the region, you could be lucky enough to see Loggerhead, Green and Hawksbill turtles – three of the planet's most endangered species.

Climate

Perpetual sun and clear blue skies sum up Dubai's weather. The emirate has a sub tropical and arid climate that gets very hot in the height of the summer. Rainfall is infrequent and normally only occurs in winter. Occasionally there are sandstorms when the sand is whipped off the desert. Temperatures range from a low of around 10°C (50°F) in winter, to a high of 48C (118°F) in summer. The mean daily maximum is 24°C (75°F) in January, rising to 41°C (106°F) in August.

Trading hub

While Dubai is not the country's capital city (that honour is bestowed upon neighbouring Abu Dhabi) it is the most liberal of the emirates and perhaps even the most exciting and free-thinking in the Arabian

Gulf. Less than a century ago it was little more than a hub for pearl diving and Bedouin traders, but its location and relative proximity to Europe, India, Africa and the Far East has always been its strength. And since the discovery, and later the exportation of oil, it's taken full advantage. With over 25 million passengers passing through Dubai international airport last year, there's still much more to come from this emirate of just 3,885 square kilometres.

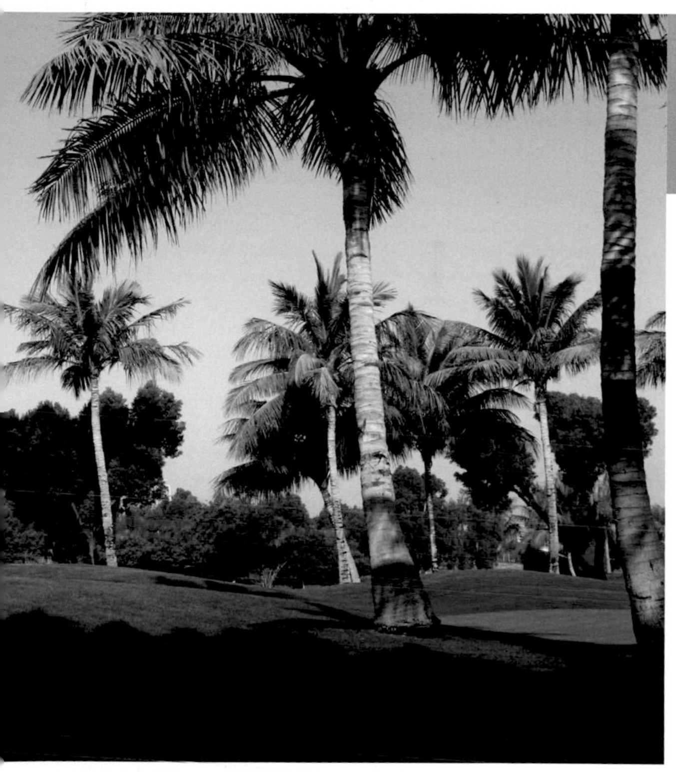

History in the making

The history of Dubai is an intriguing rags-to-riches tale. A story of pirates and pearl divers, of villainy, colony and independence, told in double-quick time.

Historical documentation of Dubai is scarce, but the city's emphatic position as the region's leading trading post dates back to the ancient Kingdom of Sumer around 3000 BC. There are even records that link the emirate to the Bronze Age Magan civilisation of 2000 BC, and suggest that Dubai Port was the main shipping route between Oman and Mesopotamia, as well as other ancient empires.

The list of occupiers from 3000 BC onwards was swift, with one civilisation overcoming and conquering the last. Among the most influential was the Persian dynasty of Sassanid, who had taken Dubai Creek and its surrounding areas as its own since 224 BC. But it was a short-lived occupation. Come the seventh century, the Umayyads came, settled, and bought with them Islam from western Saudi Arabia.

The Arabs were followed by the Mongols and soon after the Ottomons, each leaving their mark on the local culture and all championing the Islamic religion.

From the eighth century onwards, Dubai strengthened its position as a leading trade port between the eastern and western worlds, with the silk trade from China and the pearling industry of the Persian Gulf earning

the region some major maritime brownie points. In particular, both the British and Portuguese looked to the region as a strategic gateway between Europe and India. The prosperous trade route attracted attention from some less than appealing characters, however, and incidents of pirate hijackings became prevalent enough to earn the area the title of 'Pirate Coast'.

But that didn't stop trade and sometime in the 16th century the Portuguese attempted to claim the land as their own. The move backfired, however, when the Bedouin tribes and local inhabitants fled the coast and moved further inland. It wasn't long before the British seized control of the waterways, put an end to piracy and formed a treaty with the rulers to establish the Trucial States. It was to be the start of a bitter story of local tribal power struggles, deeply embroiled in British imperial dreams.

By the early 1800s, Dubai's growing reputation as a trading epicentre attracted the attention of the local Bani Yas tribe, who, under the leadership of Maktoum bin Butti (father of the Al Maktoum dynasty that

Development of Islam

Dubai's early existence is closely linked to the growth of Islam in the greater Middle East region. The religion developed in modern-day Saudi Arabia at the beginning of the seventh century AD with the revelations of the Quran being received by the Prophet Mohammed. Military conquests of the Middle East and North Africa enabled the Arab empire to spread teachings of Islam from Mecca and Medina to the local Bedouin tribes.

Dubai ruling family tree

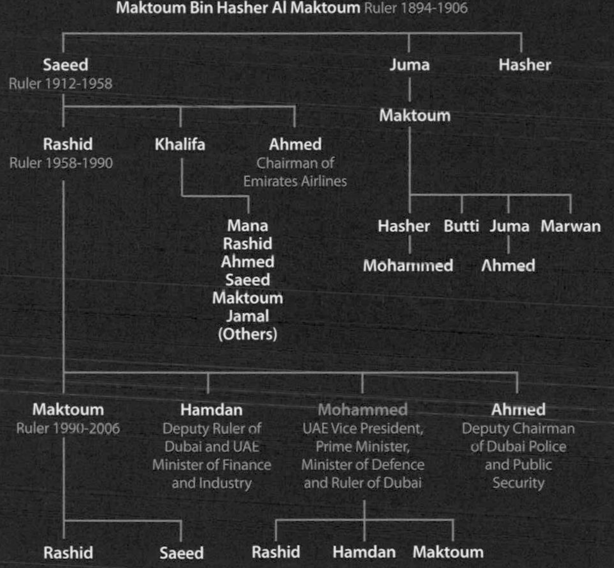
Maktoum Bin Hasher Al Maktoum Ruler 1894-1906
Saeed
Ruler 1912-1958
Juma
Hasher
Maktoum
Rashid
Ruler 1958-1990
Khalifa
Ahmed
Chairman of
Emirates Airlines
Mana
Rashid
Ahmed
Saeed
Maktoum
Jamal
(Others)
Hasher
Butti
Juma
Marwan
Mohammed
Ahmed
Maktoum
Ruler 1990-2006
Hamdan
Deputy Ruler of
Dubai and UAE
Minister of Finance
and Industry
Mohammed
UAE Vice President,
Prime Minister,
Minister of Defence
and Ruler of Dubai
Ahmed
Deputy Chairman
of Dubai Police
and Public
Security
Rashid
Saeed
Rashid
Hamdan
Maktoum

still runs the show today), moved and reclaimed the town as its own. Business boomed under Sheikh Maktoum and before long Dubai was the region's leading trading hub. To strengthen this position, Sheikh Maktoum established tax exemption laws for foreign traders and Dubai's momentum gathered pace.

The Trucial States, who had granted the British control over foriegn affairs in an earlier agreement, formed an alliance that would eventually lead to the formation of independent states. In 1971, the United Arab Emirates was born, initially comprising Abu Dhabi, Ajman, Dubai, Fujairah, Sharjah, Umm Al Quwain, with Ras Al Khaimah joining in 1972. Under the agreement, individual emirates each retained a certain degree of autonomy, with Abu Dhabi and Dubai providing the most drive to the federation. The rulers chose Sheikh Zayed bin Sultan Al Nahyan, the leader of Abu Dhabi, to be President of the UAE, a position he held until his death in November 2004. Sheikh Zayed was much-loved and considered a people's ruler, and it was under his reign which begain in 1966 that the country finally exploited its rich oil reserves, discovered 10 years earlier under the reign of his brother, Sheikh Shakhbut.

Abu Dhabi was transformed from one of the poorest states to one of the richest in the

An admired ruler

The late Sheikh Zayed bin Sultan Al Nahyan was revered by his peers and adored by the public. Over the 33 years of his rule he was responsible for major developments to the region's economy, and was the pioneer of extending privileges to expatriates, from job opportunities to property-buying power.

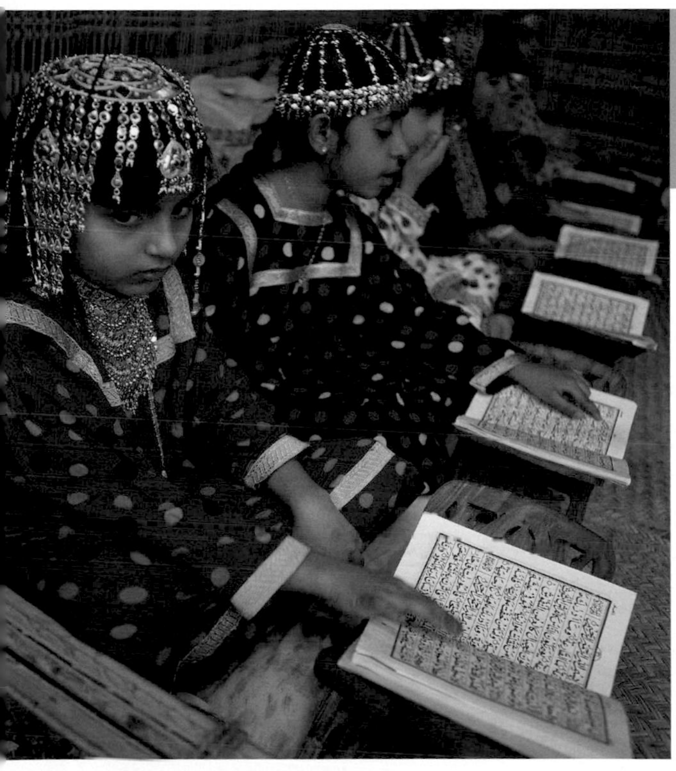

world (Abu Dhabi holds a staggering 10% of the world's known oil reserves). In 1966, Dubai followed suit and began mining its own oil. While the emirate was always a relatively wealthy trading centre, its riches now boomed. Sheikh Rashid Saeed Al Maktoum was ruler of Dubai when oil was discovered. When he died in 1990, his son, Sheikh Maktoum bin Rashid, took over. Sheikh Rashid is credited with using the oil revenue to develop Dubai, and this work has been continued by his sons, including present ruler, Sheikh Mohammed Bin Rashid Al Maktoum. But such has been the country's economic development that oil now accounts for just a small percentage of Dubai's GDP.

UAE and Dubai timeline

3000 BC – Dubai, or Deira in particular, serves as a key trading post in the ancient Persian Gulf kingdom of Sumer.
2000 BC – Bronze Age Magan Civilisation uses the port of Dubai as an important trade route.
224 BC – The Persian Dynasty of Sassanids are driven out by the Umayyads, who bring the religion of Islam from neighbouring Saudi Arabia. They are followed by the Mongol and Ottomans.
1766 – British gain control of the region's waterways.
1833 – Bani Yas tribe move and settle in Dubai and the Al Maktoum dynasty is born.
1892 – Sheikh Maktoum bin Butti signs exclusive business deal to allow British fleets through Dubai waters.
1894 – Sheikh Maktoum bin Butti permits full tax exemption for all foreign traders.
1966 – Commercial quantities of oil discovered.
1971 – The UAE becomes a six-emirate independent state.
1972 – Ras Al Khaimah joins to complete the UAE, and Sheikh Zayed bin Sultan Al Nahyan, leader of Abu Dhabi, takes on the role as president of the UAE.
2004 – Sheikh Zayed bin Sultan Al Nahyan dies and is succeeded by his son as ruler of the UAE, Sheikh Khalifa bin Zayed Al Nayhan.
2006 – Sheikh Maktoum bin Rashid Al Maktoum dies and is succeeded by his brother, Sheikh Mohammed bin Rashid Al Maktoum, as the ruler of Dubai.

Tradition and culture

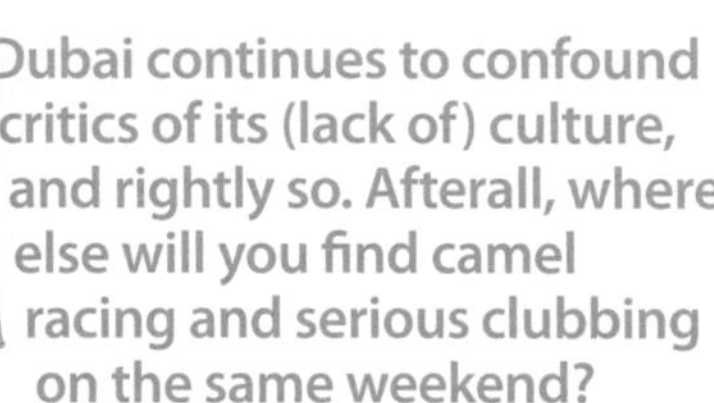

Dubai continues to confound critics of its (lack of) culture, and rightly so. Afterall, where else will you find camel racing and serious clubbing on the same weekend?

Dubai manages what many other Arab cities fail to achieve, a healthy and hearty balance between western influence and eastern tradition. Its culture is still very much rooted in Islamic traditions that deeply penetrate the Arabian Peninsula and beyond, but the city's visionary development is proof positive of an open-minded and liberal outlook.

Thanks to its geographical position as the region's trading and business hub and, more recently, its role as tourist hot-spot, Dubai has consistently encouraged open-mindedness in order to strengthen its attraction to investors and travellers (for example, the city does not share the practices concerning women as some of its more conservative neighbours). All this said and done, the rulers of the Emirates are still very active in preserving the country's heritage and safeguarding the culture from erosion and the negative influence of tourism.

Visitors can expect to be charmed by the genuine warmth and friendliness of the people here. And there's no way that you're going to miss the distinct sense of national pride that is prevalent. It's incredibly common, for example, to see locals in their traditional dress. For the men this is a dishdash(a) or

khandura – a full-length shirt-dress that is worn with a white or red chequered headdress (gutra) and secured in place with black cord (agal). Women wear a black abaya – a long, loose black robe that opens from the front.

Religion and Ramadan

Islam is the official religion in the UAE and is widely practised. The religion is based on five pillars (Faith, Prayer, Charity, Fasting and Pilgrimage) and Muslims are called upon to pray five times a day, though these times vary according to the position of the sun. It is worth keeping in mind that Islam serves as more than just a religion and is the basis for a complete way of life that all locals and Muslim expats adhere to. There are plenty of mosques dotted around the city and while most people pray in them, it's not unusual to see people kneeling by the side of the road if they are not near a mosque. Keep in mind that it's considered incredibly impolite to stare at people praying and offensive to walk over their prayer mats. Friday is the Islamic holy day and some shops and malls will be closed or will at least shut down around lunchtime in accordance with state and Islamic law.

Arabic family names

Names are usually taken from an important person in the Quran or the person's tribe. This is followed by the word bin (son of) for a boy, or bint (daughter of) for a girl, and then the name of the child's father. The last name indicates the person's tribe or family. For prominent families, this has Al, the Arabic word for 'the', before it.

Overview

The holy month of Ramadan is 30 days of abstinence where followers fast from all food, drink, cigarettes and unclean thoughts/activities from dawn to dusk. Since the month is not fixed in any way to western calendars, a little research is well worth it. Non-Muslims are obliged, out of respect, to refrain from eating, drinking or smoking in public areas during the fasting hours. Office hours are also cut, parks and shops open and close later, and entertainment, such as live music, is stopped and cinemas limit daytime screenings. Eid Al Fitr (Feast of The Breaking of the Fast) is a three-day celebration and holiday that ends the month of Ramadan, and has similar connotations as Diwali has for Hindus and Christmas for Christians.

Cuisine and shisha

From sidewalk stands serving mouth-watering shawarma (lamb or chicken sliced from a spit) and falafel (mashed and fried chickpea balls) to the more elaborate Ghuzi (whole roast lamb on a bed of rice and mixed nuts), there are plenty of opportunites to sample Arabic favourites in Dubai. You'll find a host of fine Lebanese and Arabic restuarants throughout the city (see p152).

Pork products are still a no-go for a lot of restaurants, so don't be shocked if you don't find the meat on some menus. Alcohol is considered with a little more leniency but is still only served in licensed outlets associated with hotels, and only a handful of clubs.

Coffee is a big deal in the Middle East and is an important ritual of hospitality here. The Emirates has its own flavour of 'gahwa' (that's coffee to you and me), which is very mild with a distinct flavour of cardamom and saffron, served black, never with sugar and instead sweetened with mouthfuls of delicious dates. It's respectful to have about three small cups (keep the numbers odd, it's more polite) and don't sup up every last drop (the dregs are not for consumption). Be warned, it's nigh on a cardinal sin to refuse a cup of coffee as it's taken as refusing your host's generosity.

You are also more than likely going to see a lot of shisha smoking while you are here. Ubiquitous in the Middle East, the fruity flavoured water pipe, more properly known as nargile, is a popular way to get together with friends and unwind after a hard day's slog, or shopping. It can be smoked with a variety of aromatic flavours, such as strawberry, grape and apple.

Dubai today

The world's biggest theme park, the world's tallest building, and then, simply, The World. Sometimes Dubai really does feel like a different planet.

When it comes to jaw-droppingly vast new builds, this city just can't help itself. If there's a brand new skyscraper to be built, Dubai will make sure it's the most expensive and spectacular structure ever seen. Run out of coastline? No problem. Dubai will fund and build record-breaking, man-made islands in the shapes of palms and whole planets. Driver-less metro trains, impossibly big theme parks and a replica of The Forbidden City – the list of Dubai's fantastically ambitious projects just goes on...

Burj Dubai

www.burjdubai.com

Already under construction, Burj Dubai promises to be the tallest structure in the world. And while its actual height is a closely guarded secret, the rumour is that it will be higher than the proposed Freedom Tower in New York and will dwarf Dubai's current record breaker, the Emirates Office Tower on Sheikh Zayed Road. Nearby will be Dubai Mall and its nine million feet of retail, residential and entertainment amenities, including the world's biggest gold souk, an IMAX cinema and even an Olympic-sized ice rink.

Height Top secret, but estimated to be around 700 metres
Completion 2008

The World

Burj Dubai

Space and Science World

Dubai Festival City www.dubaifestivalcity.com

A 4km stretch of prime creek-side real estate will become a resort-style city that will include housing, shopping, a marina and an 18-hole golf course, designed by the world renowned Robert Trent Jones II. The Middle East's biggest IKEA is already open on the same site.

Size 3.8 kilometres

Completion Entire project will be completed by 2015

Dubai International Airport www.dubaiairport.com

Already recognised as the aviation hub of the Middle East, Dubai International Airport sees some serious traffic, accommodating some 100 airlines flying to over 140 destinations worldwide. Construction is underway on the third terminal, with the airport hoping to handle 70 million passengers per year by 2016 and 100 million per year by 2025.

Capacity 70 million passengers a year

Completion 2007

Dubailand www.dubailand.ae

Featuring six themed worlds and over 200 leisure and entertainment projects, this beast makes Disney look like a village fun fair. The brochure alone is enough to make adults, never mind kids, tingle with excitement – theme parks, museums, galleries, spa resorts, sports academies (including a Manchester United Soccer School) are all part of the masterplan.

Size 3 billion square feet

Completion Phase one expected in 2008

Dubai Metro/Railway Project

With Dubai (and its population) growing at a dramatic rate, the lack of an alternative to commuting by car is threatening to bring the city to a standstill. In response, Dubai Metro is proposing a fleet of over 100 driver-less electric trains operating above and below ground. The total of the two lines will be nearly 70km long, with 35 stations along the line that will stretch from Sheikh Zayed Road to Jebel Ale. The cost? A mere US$4 billion.

Size 29 stations across the city

Completion 2009 at the earliest

Dubai Waterfront

www.dubaiwaterfront.ae

Dwarfing all previous developments, the Waterfront will consist of over 250 individual communities. Madinat Al Arab, another new 'downtown' will feature Al Burj – yet another one of the world's tallest buildings. Phase one sold out (to selected developers) within five days – for a cool Dhs.13 billion.

Size 81 square kilometres, it will add 850km of new coastline

Completion First phase by 2010

Dubai World Central

Another world record breaker, this city will be centred around the massive Dubai World Central International Airport, which, once complete, will have the same capacity as London's Heathrow. The development will eventually house around 750,000 people in an area twice the size of Hong Kong Island.

Size 140 square kilometres

Completion Not known

Sport City at Dubailand

Jumeirah Beach Residence

www.jbr.ae

Just when you thought Dubai couldn't squeeze another self-contained community along its seafront, along come the folks at JBR with perhaps the final piece of luxury on the last bit of natural coastline. Once complete there will be a whopping 36 residential towers housing 6,500 apartments.

Size 2.043 Km^2

Completion Early 2007

The Palm Islands

www.thepalm.ae

The much-hyped palms are adding a phenomenal amount of extra coastline and construction to Dubai, as well as providing some of the most extravagant home addresses on the planet to David Beckham et al. The Palm Jumeirah alone will house close to 7,000 apartments.

Size Trunk lengths: Jumeirah – 2km, Deira - 2.9km, Jebel Ali – 2.4km

Completion Jumerirah, end of 2006

The World

www.theworld.ae

Nakheel is well into a US1.8billion project to create 300 islands that will eventually resemble the shape of the world. Built four kilometres offshore, each island will be sold as a private retreat, with Hawaii yours for a few million dirhams.

Size 9km east to west x 6km north to south

Completion 2007

Exploring

Whatever next?

You've read about five-star hotels, limitless luxury and never-ending skyscrapers. Now it's time for the rest of the story...

Amid the commotion and cliche surrounding this compelling city, there is a side that's rarely seen or heard. Never mind the growth spurts and gonzo shopping malls, what about its ancient traditions, its cosmopolitan residents, its spectacular coastline?

To find the answers, you need to take advantage of Dubai's unique location and explore life beyond its luxury hotels and legendary bling. After all, when's the last time you jumped on a sand board, or camped in the desert? Or took to water for some of the best snorkelling and diving in the Arabian Gulf? Dubai's warm winters make all this and much more – from kitesurfing to waterskiing – possible.

Away from the bright lights of the city, there are beautiful, natural landscapes to discover. You are just a short car journey or flight from the capital of the UAE, Abu Dhabi, and the nearby Liwa Oasis (p.107), as well as the breathtaking and historically rich Sultanate of Oman (p.112). Then there's the rugged Hajar mountains of the east coast and the rare beauty of Mussandam (p.103).

Back in Dubai, you only have to take an abra (water taxi) ride across the creek to find that the city's heartbeat is still where early settlers built their huts – along the gleaming stretch of water that divides the city in two: Deira to the north and Bur Dubai to the south. It's a rare example of demarcation in a city that lacks traditional boundaries. This, combined with the absence of decent public transport, means that you'll navigate Dubai a little differently. But come on, what did you expect?

This chapter has been divided into the city's most popular areas, each with a detailed map pinpointing the main attractions, sights and landmarks.

There's a quick reference page in each section detailing the best choices for relaxation, eating, drinking, families and sightseeing in the area. And use the pull-out map of Dubai at the back of the book to track down the must-dos listed on page 34.

With a dizzying array of new developments underway in Dubai – be it the world's tallest building or a Manhattan-sized man-made Island – it's sometimes hard to keep track of this city's shifting sands, but don't worry – the following pages cover all the latest projects, as well as the best of what this incredible city has to offer.

Outside Dubai

The other countries of the Gulf Cooperation Council (GCC) are well worth a visit, especially if you want to get a fuller picture of the traditions and culture of the Middle East. Whether you want to catch the Asian Games in Qatar, check out the colourful heritage of Kuwait or discover the tranquility of Oman, there is plenty to explore. Each country is just a short, cheap flight from Dubai.

Dubai essentials

Abra Ride (Water Taxi)

Pull-out map 1-F2, ref 1

Dubai's cheapest form of public transport, and its most charming, costs just Dhs.1 to cross the creek (rumours are it may rise to Dhs.3!). To explore off the official route, hire an abra for around Dhs.50 per hour. **See p.49**

Bastakiya

Pull-out map 1-E2, ref 2

Bastakiya's traditional four-sided windtowers not only give a glimpse of old-school air conditioning but overlook narrow, atmospheric alleyways full of museums, galleries and shops – a breath of fresh air. **See p.42**

Burj Al Arab

Pull-out map 2-D1, ref 3

Stunning inside and out, the billowing sail doesn't disappoint. Indulge yourself with afternoon tea at Sahn Eddar, cocktails at Sky View, or take a simulated submarine ride to the seafood restaurant, Al Mahara. **See p.84**

Desert Safari

Off map

Whether you want to surf the dunes in a car, ride a camel, sand ski, learn to belly dance or simply stare out over a sea of sand at sunset, a trip into the desert is a must during your time in Dubai. **See p.93**

Dinner Cruise

Pull-out map 1-F2, ref 4

No ordinary journey up river, an evening cruise in Dubai is the best way to take in the sights and sounds of Bur Dubai and Deira from the comfort of the dinner table – with shisha pipe in hand., of course. **See p.49**

Dubai Museum

Pull-out map 1-E2, ref 5

It's virtually impossible to picture Dubai before the hectic high-rise invasion, but with the help of the expertly curated exhibitions at Dubai Museum, you'll soon get a feel for the simple life once led in the UAE. **See p.40**

Heritage & Diving Village

Pull-out map 1-E1, ref 6

What was once the fishing village of Shindagha is now home to a number of sensitively restored buildings, including museums offering a rare chance to see traditional crafts, tribal dances and ceremonies. **See p.40**

Jumeirah Mosque

Pull-out map 1-B1, ref 7

Aside from its beauty, especially when lit at night, this mosque is also one of the few in the UAE which non-Muslims are able to enter. Organised tours are held on Sunday and Thursday mornings at 10:00 sharp. **See p.61**

Souk Madinat

Pull-out map 2-D2, ref 8

Styled on a traditional souk (albeit one with air conditioning) the Madinat is a maze of craft shops, cafes and charming waterfront bars and restaurants. Oh, and it has two five-star hotels just for good measure. **See p.84**

Ski Dubai

Pull-out map 2-D2, ref 9

Despite its novelty location in a shopping mall, there is serious skiing and snowboarding to be had on the Middle East's only fake slopes (there's even a black run for show-offs). Head to the beach afterwards to warm up. **See p.87**

Souks

Pull-out map 1-F1, ref 10

More slow-paced than the majority of the Middle East's traditional markets, Dubai's souks come in three main flavours – Gold, Spice and Textile – and each one is not to be missed. Head for the creek and haggle. **See p.48**

Wild Wadi Water Park

Pull-out map 2-D1, ref 11

Be warned: you may end up loving this over-sized waterpark more than your kids. It's the biggest outside North America and boasts a truly terryfying plunge in the shape of the *Jumeirah Sceirah*. **See p.86**

Bur Dubai & Karama

Whoever says Dubai is short of history and heritage clearly hasn't spent any time in this part of town.

Bordering the creek to the north, Bur Dubai is where past and present combine to create an atmosphere unmatched in the city. Dubai Municipality has made a concerted effort to create an area of cultural heritage and significance here and it shows – wander its streets and you'll get a fresh perspective on the emirate and its pre-oil past. *For **restaurants and bars** in the area, see p.156.*

Sheikh Saeed Al Maktoum's House

04 393 7139

Next to Heritage & Diving Village www.dubaitourism.ae

Near the mouth of the creek in Shindagha, you'll find the one-time home of Dubai's much-loved former ruler, and grandfather of Sheikh Mohammed bin Rashid Al Maktoum. Recently restored, the modest house-turned-museum (which dates back to 1896) is a fine example of a traditional Arabian building with its separate entrances for men and women and windtower in the majlis (main living area). It also provides an intriguing insight into the emirate's history through a series of displays and rare photographs, including an extensive range of currencies which preceded the dirham.

Entrance fees: Adults Dhs.2; children Dhs.1; under 5 years free.

Timings: Saturday-Thursday: 08-20.30; Friday: 15.30-21.30

Map A 1

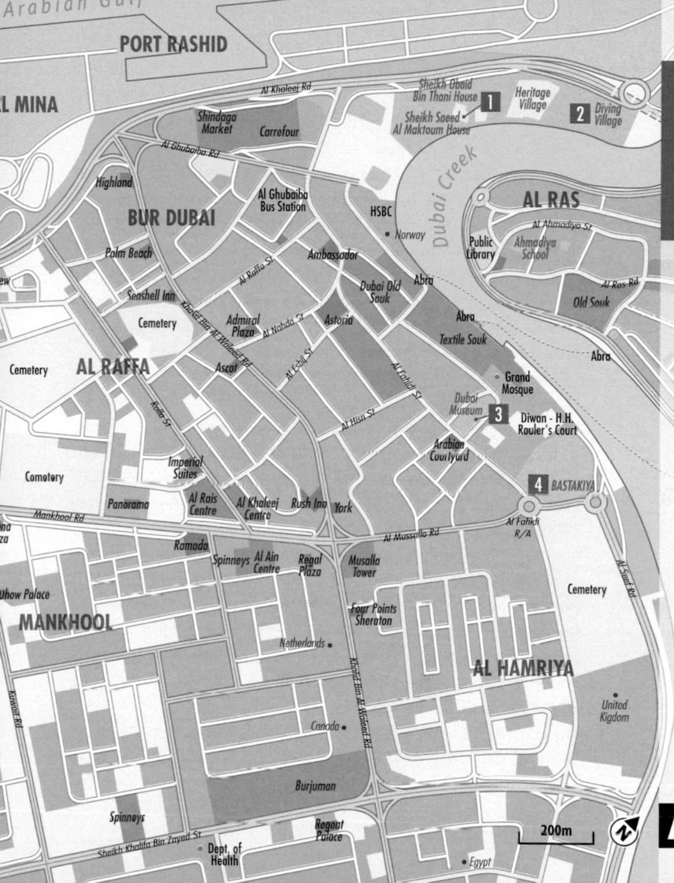
Arabian Gulf
PORT RASHID
L MINA
Al Khaleej Rd
Sheikh Obaid Bin Thani House
1
Heritage Village
2
Diving Village
Sheikh Saeed Al Maktoum House
Shindaga Market
Carrefour
Al Ghubaiba Rd
Dubai Creek
Highland
Al Ghubaiba Bus Station
HSBC
AL RAS
BUR DUBAI
Norway
Al Ahmadiya St
Public Library
Ahmadiya School
Palm Beach
Ambassador
Al Raffa St
Dubai Old Souk
Abra
Al Ras Rd
Seashell Inn
Old Souk
Khalid Bin Al Waleed Rd
Cemetery
Admiral Plaza
Al Nahda St
Astoria
Abra
Textile Souk
Abra
Cemetery
AL RAFFA
Ascot
Al Esbij St
Al Fahidi St
Grand Mosque
Dubai Museum
3
Diwan - H.H. Ruler's Court
Rolla St
Al Hisn St
Arabian Courtyard
Imperial Suites
Cemetery
4
BASTAKIYA
Panorama
Al Rais Centre
Al Khaleej Centre
Rush Inn
York
Mankhool Rd
Al Fahidi R/A
Al Mussalla Rd
Ramada
Spinneys
Al Ain Centre
Regal Plaza
Musalla Tower
Al Seef Rd
Cemetery
Dhow Palace
MANKHOOL
Four Points Sheraton
Netherlands
Khalid Bin Al Waleed Rd
AL HAMRIYA
Kuwait Rd
United Kigdom
Canada
Burjuman
Spinneys
Regent Palace
200m
Sheikh Khalifa Bin Zayed St
Dept. of Health
Egypt
N

Heritage & Diving Village

04 393 7151

Nr Shindagha Tunnel www.dubaitourism.ae

Wind your way a little further around the creek and you'll come across this homage to Dubai's pearl diving traditions and maritime past. All the buildings have been renovated and restored to recreate traditional life in Dubai before the middle of the last century, but the main focus of the Village is the museum, where you can watch resident potters practise a craft that has survived for centuries. This is also one of the few places where you can see local women serving traditionally cooked Emirati bread. Souvenirs are also on sale, and camel rides are available most afternoons and evenings. Map A 2

Dubai Museum

04 353 1862

Nr Bastakiya www.dubaitourism.ae

Located within one of the city's oldest buildings (Al Fahedi Fort), Dubai Museum is a must-see. The fort was originally built as the ruler's residence and to protect the city from invasion, but was renovated in the early 90s and turned into a museum. It vividly depicts everyday life before the discovery of oil, with galleries recreating a souk from the 1950s, a stroll through an oasis complete with falaj, and the marine life of the UAE. Opposite the museum is the 'Diwan', the highest administrative body of the Dubai government. Nearby you'll find the spectacular Grand Mosque with its 54 domes and 70 metre minaret. Map A 3

Museum entrance fees: Adults Dhs.3; children under 10 Dhs.1.
Timings: Saturday-Thursday: 0800-22:00; Friday 08:00-11:00 and 16:00-20:00

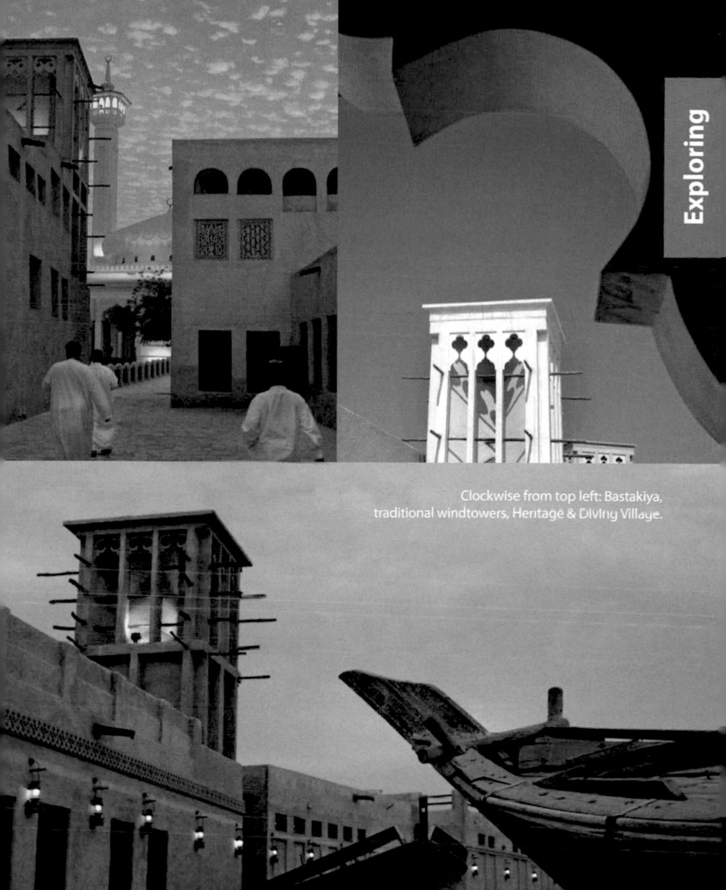

Clockwise from top left: Bastakiya, traditional windtowers, Heritage & Diving Village.

Bastakiya

Between Diwan R/A and Fahedi R/A

The oldest heritage site in the city and arguably its most charming and atmospheric, Bastakiya dates back to the early 1900s and is characterised by traditional windtower ('barjeel' in Arabic) houses, built around courtyards and clustered together around a winding maze of alleyways. Many buildings here have been restored and converted into art galleries, shops, cafes and offices (including the Sheikh Mohammed Centre for Cultural Understanding). Map A 4

The Majlis Gallery

04 353 6233

Al Fahedi St

www.majlisgallery.com

Set in a traditional house in Bastakiya, the small whitewashed rooms of the Majlis lead off to a central garden area and host a

variety of exhibitions by contemporary artists throughout the year. A range of fine art, hand-made glass, pottery, fabrics, frames are on sale. Map A 4

XVA Gallery

04 353 5383

Bastakiya

Located in the centre of Bastakiya, the XVA Gallery is one of Dubai's best exhibition spaces. The fully restored house is worth visiting for its architecture and displays of local and international art, or for a snack in its tranquil courtyard. The gallery focuses mainly on paintings and hosts exhibitions throughout the year. There are eight guestrooms on the upper floors should you want to stay a little longer in this part of town. Map A 4

Karama

It's fair to say that there are only two factors which will draw you to Karama during your stay in Dubai. The first will be found in the Karama Shopping Complex, the second in one of its good restaurants serving tasty and cheap cuisine.

Karama's open-air shopping area is a great place for buying anything from 'designer' clothes and handbags to kitsch fluffy camels and even silver jewellery from Oman. Just be aware of the incessant approaches from vendors offering you good prices on that 'special' Rolex.

Karama's restaurants on the other hand are no hassle at all, with a choice of extremely good Arabic and Indian, as well as Sri Lankan and Singaporean eateries. Favourites include Gazebo and Karachi Darbar.

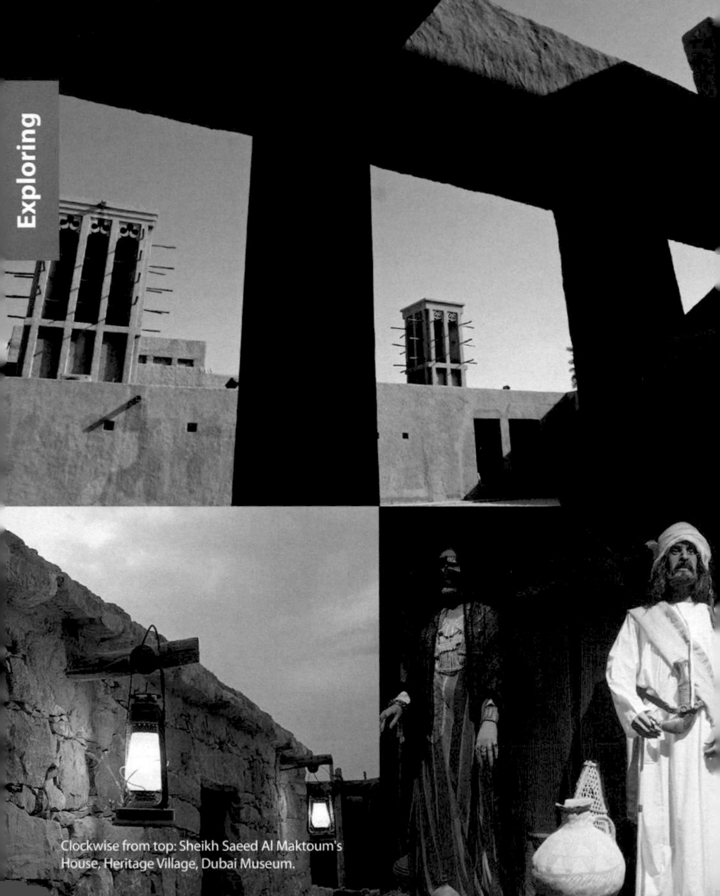

Clockwise from top: Sheikh Saeed Al Maktoum's House, Heritage Village, Dubai Museum.

If you only do one thing in...

Bur Dubai & Karama

Head to Dubai Museum and find out what life was like before the malls and madding crowds.

Best for...

eating and drinking Finish a hard day's sightseeing with a bite at Karachi Darbar (p.159), one of Karama's Pakistani restaurants.

sightseeing The winding alleyways of Bastakiya (p.42) will linger in the memory long after you leave Dubai.

shopping Tough call, but cheap and cheerful Karama (p.43) wins out over the designer chic of BurJuman (p.136).

relaxation Enjoy a snack or coffee in the tranquil courtyard of the fine art gallery, Majlis, or its neighbour, XVA (p.43).

families Head for the Diving and Heritage Village (p.40), where the kids can hop on a camel while you stuff yourself with freshly baked bread.

Deira & the creek

Old town Dubai is an atmospheric blend of heritage and modernity, where breathtaking architecture overlooks the city's oldest souks.

From the dhow wharfage to Deira's numerous souks, this is a slice of creek life that you won't want to miss. Before skyscrapers and luxury spas moved in, this was city life: narrow, bustling streets, full of the scent of spices and the glint of gold. Today it's still one of the most bustling areas of the city. And the hustle remains addictive.

Before you soak up 'old' Dubai, take a look at the awe-inspiring buildings bordering the creek. The eclectic mix of hotels, public and commercial structures showcase some of the city's most imaginative architecture, and three of Dubai's top five-star hotels, Hilton Dubai Creek, Sheraton Dubai Creek, and the SAS Radisson Dubai Creek, can be found here.

Further along the creek, the wharfage offers a rare glimpse of Dubai's trading history and local merchant life. While the bulk of imported and exported goods moves through the modern ports along the coast, here you will see everything from fruit and vegetables to televisions and cars being unloaded on the dock. Deira's reputation for traffic is legendary, so try to visit either mid-morning or mid-afternoon. There is, of course, a traditional alternative to the traffic. Arrive in Deira by abra (water taxi), from Bur Dubai Abra station. *For **restaurants and bars** in the area, see p.160.*

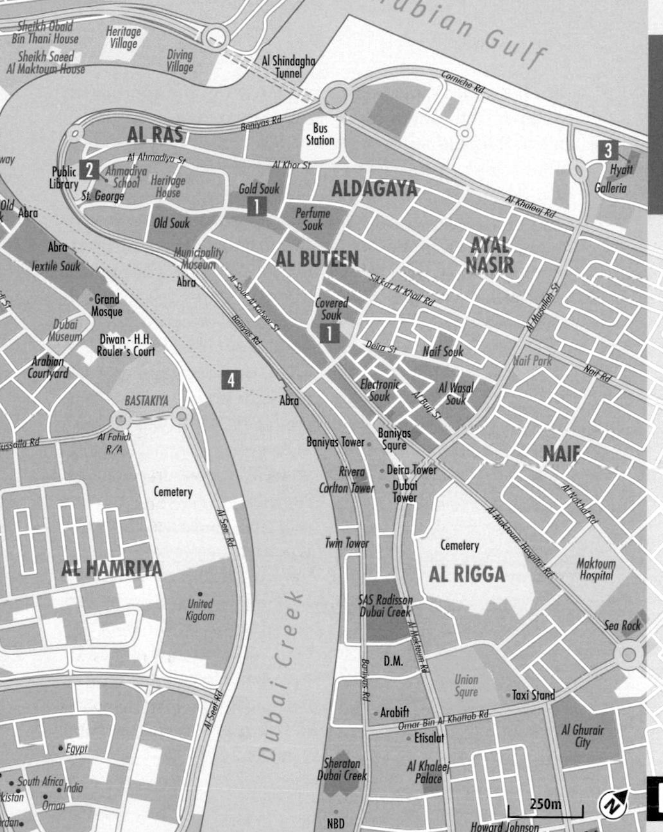
Arabian Gulf
Sheikh Obaid Bin Thani House
Heritage Village
Sheikh Saeed Al Maktoum House
Diving Village
Al Shindagha Tunnel
Corniche Rd
Baniyas Rd
Bus Station
AL RAS
Al Ahmadiya St
Al Khor St
Public Library
2
Ahmadiya School
Heritage House
St. George
Gold Souk
1
ALDAGAYA
3
Hyatt Galleria
Al Khaleej Rd
Abra
Old Souk
Perfume Souk
Abra
Textile Souk
Municipality Museum
AL BUTEEN
AYAL NASIR
Abra
Al Souk Al Kabeer St
Sikkat Al Khail Rd
Grand Mosque
Covered Souk
1
Al Musallah St
Dubai Museum
Baniyas Rd
Diwan - H.H. Rouler's Court
Deira St
Naif Souk
Arabian Courtyard
Naif Park
Naif Rd
4
Electronic Souk
Al Wasal Souk
Abra
Al Buij St
BASTAKIYA
Al Fahidi R/A
Al Mussalla Rd
Baniyas Squre
Baniyas Tower
NAIF
Rivera
Deira Tower
Carlton Tower
Dubai Tower
Cemetery
Al Nakhal Rd
Al Seef Rd
Al Maktoum Hospital Rd
Twin Tower
Cemetery
AL HAMRIYA
AL RIGGA
Maktoum Hospital
United Kigdom
SAS Radisson Dubai Creek
Sea Rock
Dubai Creek
Al Maktoum Rd
D.M.
Baniyas Rd
Union Squre
Taxi Stand
Al Seef Rd
Arabift
Omar Bin Al Khattab Rd
Al Ghurair City
Etisalat
Egypt
Sheraton Dubai Creek
Al Khaleej Palace
South Africa
India
Pakistan
Oman
250m
Jordan
NBD
Howard Johnson
Lords
Safir

Deira souks

Al Buteen

Take the pedestrian underpass to the left of the abra station to enter the oldest and most atmospheric markets in Dubai. The Gold Souk, the Spice Souk and Deira Old Souk in Al Ras give you a great impression of why trade used to be more of an artform. You won't get anywhere here without bargaining skills and cold, hard cash. But go armed with a smile and a good sense of theatre and you might just match the vendors at their own game. The Gold Souk (p.163) needs little introduction, with its row upon row of shops selling yellow and white gold, silver and platinum, all designed to wipe out your holiday budget in one go. Nearby is the aromatherapy delights of the Spice Souk, where you'll find every imaginable spice, as well as loose frankincense, perfumed oils and dried herbs sold for medicinal purposes. When it comes to bargaining in the souks, make sure you're laid-back and vaguely disinterested, however much you want the item. Your initial bid should be between 50% and 75% of what the vendor is offering. When this is rejected, just keep on haggling... Map B 1

Gridlock Deira

It's a good idea to leave the hire car at home when you visit Deira. The traffic here is probably worse than anywhere else in Dubai; congestion over Garhoud Bridge is horrendous and can sometimes triple your normal journey time. Even short trips can be tricky. Need more convincing to get a cab? Parking's awful, too.

Al Ahmadiya School

04 226 0286
Al Khor St, Al Ras
www.dubaitourism.ae

Heading further towards the sea, set back a little from the main roads by the creek, is a small area being renovated by Dubai Municipality. It contains the earliest school in the city, Al Ahmadiya School (now the Museum of Education), while one of the area's other buildings, renovated in the last few years, has been turned into a traditionally styled courtyard with a hotel and an old-style mosque. Map B 2

Hyatt Regency Hotel

04 209 1234
Nr Gold Souk
www.dubai.regency.hyatt.com

The Hyatt, one of Dubai's first five-star hotels, has great views over the mouth of the creek and out to sea, particularly from Al Dawaar, the city's only revolving restaurant. This is the best spot to see The Palm Deira, which is famously set to cover a distance almost as large as Greater London and bigger than Paris or Manhattan. Not far from the Hyatt is Dubai's largest and busiest fish market (see p.150). It's a rare chance to see traditional tradesmen at work, and the recent addition of a musuem makes a trip more than worthwhile. Map B 3

Creek cruises and dhow charters

There's no better way to soak up the character of the city than with a trip across the creek by abra (water taxi). Not only is it incredibly cheap (between Dhs.1 and Dhs.3), it's also a good opportunity to see locals, expats and tourists coming together. If you've got the money, you can charter your own dhow for a night's sailing on the creek or further up the coast. Map B 4

Dubai Creek

If you only do one thing in...
Deira & the creek

Watch the dhows unload at the corniche, then head for a stroll around Dubai's famous souks.

Best for...

drinking and eating Grab a slice of modern life amid the old town with a bite at the highly rated Indian, Ashiana (p.160), at the Sheraton Dubai Creek.

sightseeing Head for the Hyatt Regency and a table at Al Dawaar (p.160), the city's only revolving restaurant, and enjoy fantastic views across the creek and beyond.

shopping Stroll through the glittering streets of the gold souk before soaking up the smells of the spice souk.

relaxation Pull up a seat in the courtyard of Al Ahmadiya School & Heritage House and enjoy quiet amid the Deira storm.

families Forget the congested bridges and the view from the back of the car. Your kids need to cross the creek by abra.

Garhoud & Port Saeed

Step off the plane and within minutes you'll be in the midst of some of Dubai's most popular drinking holes, not to mention a few of its finest restaurants.

North of Garhoud Bridge, between the creek and the airport lies Garhoud. Despite its proximity to circling 747s it's a much sought-after residential area, and home to the Dubai International Tennis Championships. But one glance at the traffic on and around the Bridge will tell you this isn't an entirely peaceful place. During the day when the roads are clogged and the temperatures high, there seems little to recommend a stroll around its streets. But just wait until the sun goes down and watch Garhoud come to life. *For **restaurants and bars** in the area, see p.168.*

Aviation Club

04 282 4122

Garhoud

www.aviationclub.ae

Mention Garhoud to any newcomer and they might shrug; mention the Irish Village and they'll offer a knowing smile. Thanks to its combination of live music, stunning lakeside views and, er, booze, the Village and its neighbour, Century Village are perennially popular with visitors, due in no small part to their laidback vibe. Both belong to the much larger Aviation Club, which also owns Dubai Tennis Stadium, which hosts the annual Dubai International Tennis Championships. The Club's excellent Cellar restaurant is also a great spot to unwind following that tense morning in traffic. Map C 1

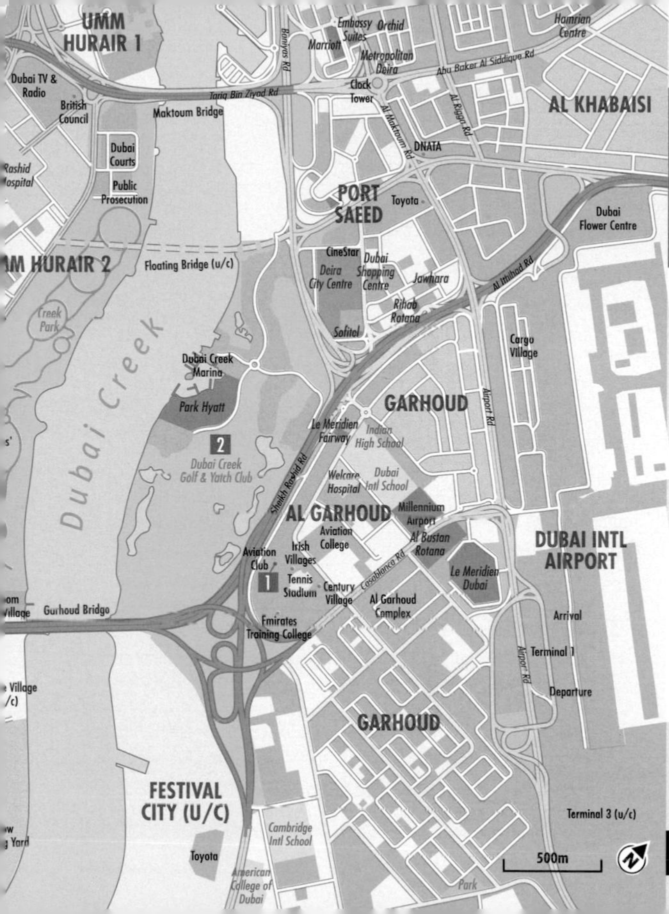

UMM HURAIR 1
Embassy Suites
Orchid
Marriott
Metropolitan Deira
Hamrian Centre
Baniyas Rd
Abu Baker Al Siddique Rd
Dubai TV & Radio
British Council
Tariq Bin Ziyad Rd
Clock Tower
AL KHABAISI
Maktoum Bridge
Al Maktoum Rd
Al Rigga Rd
Dubai Courts
DNATA
Rashid Hospital
Public Prosecution
PORT SAEED
Toyota
Dubai Flower Centre
UMM HURAIR 2
Floating Bridge (u/c)
CineStar
Deira City Centre
Dubai Shopping Centre
Jawhara
Al Ittihad Rd
Creek Park
Rihab Rotana
Sofitel
Cargo Village
Dubai Creek
Dubai Creek Marina
Park Hyatt
GARHOUD
Airport Rd
Le Meridien Fairway
Indian High School
2
Dubai Creek Golf & Yatch Club
Sheikh Rashid Rd
Welcare Hospital
Dubai Intl School
AL GARHOUD
Millennium Airport
Aviation College
Al Bustan Rotana
DUBAI INTL AIRPORT
Aviation Club
Irish Villages
Casablanca Rd
Le Meridien Dubai
1
Tennis Stadium
Century Village
Al Garhoud Complex
Garhoud Bridge
Arrival
Emirates Training College
Terminal 1
Airport Rd
Departure
GARHOUD
FESTIVAL CITY (U/C)
Terminal 3 (u/c)
Cambridge Intl School
Toyota
500m
American College of Dubai
Park
C

Park Hyatt

Dubai Creek Golf & Yacht Club

04 295 6000
Opp. Deira City Centre Mall
www.dubaigolf.com

North of the Aviation Club, you'll be struck by the rich, manicured greenery of the Dubai Creek Golf & Yacht Club. You'll know that you're in the right place when you spot a wonky Sydney Opera House. That'll be the Yacht Clubhouse.

There are any number of good bars and restaurants from which to choose, but one stands out, literally, from the rest. Boardwalk (p.168) offers some of Dubai's most spectacular and memorable views. Built on wooden stilts over the creek, the restaurant is as close as you'll get to the water without diving in. Grab a table outside in the cooler months to watch the twinkling dhows bob by.

Within the grounds of the golf club lies another jewel in Dubai's multi-studded crown, the city's latest five-star hotel, the Mediterranean-style Park Hyatt Hotel (p.242). The hotel's range of restaurants, including Traiteur and The Thai Kitchen (p.174), are superbly located on the creek side with cracking views, while its Amara spa rooms promise a private garden for that ever elusive rain shower (p.124). Map C 2

Golf by the Creek

If your waistline has expanded beyond all recognition then it's time to take up one of Dubai's favourite sports. And what better place for a leisurely round than in Garhoud. The course at Dubai Creek Golf and Yacht Club has recently been renovated, with a new front nine designed by Ryder Cup regular Thomas Bjorn. What's more, newcomers can learn the ropes from PGA-qualified Instructors. See p.118.

Clockwise from top: Boardwalk, Bateaux Dubai, Irish Village.

If you only do one thing in...

Garhoud & Port Saeed

Spend an afternoon, evening, or a whole day at the Irish Village. Not just another theme pub, but a Dubai institution.

Best for...

drinking and eating The Cellar at The Aviation Club (p.52). Great atmosphere, even better food and one of the best wine lists in Dubai.

sightseeing The views from Boardwalk (p.168) – the restaurant on stilts over the creek – are some of the best in city. The food's pretty fine, too.

shopping You name it and they sell it on the floors of Deira City Centre (p.136) – the city's long-standing and still much-loved mall.

relaxation Indulge yourself with the treatments at the highly rated Amara Spa at the Park Hyatt Hotel (p.242).

families Look no further than Magic Planet's bumper cars and video games at Deira City Centre.

Jumeira & Satwa

The pristine beaches and boutiques of Jumeira, and the bustling streets of Satwa, make this a must-see part of town.

Palm Beach has nothing on Jumeira. This is easily Dubai's most desirable residential area, thanks to its proximity to both beaches and boutiques. It's where the beautiful people live, or would if only they could afford the rents.

But don't fret if those supermodel looks have temporarily deserted you, there's plenty to keep you occupied aside from posing. Whether you love to shop, sunbathe or sample local culture and heritage, Jumeria is the place to do it. *For **restaurants and bars** in the area, see p.176.*

Jumeira Beach Park

04 349 2555

Nr Jumeirah Beach Club

www.dm.gov.ae

This is a stunning one-kilometre stretch of golden sand, littered with palm trees, and plenty of grassy areas on which to loll around. There are cafes, showers, landscaped gardens and barbecue pits for those lazy winter weekends. You can hire a sunbed and parasol for Dhs.20, but they do run out so get down early. Lifeguards man the beach from 08:00 to sunset, when swimming is not permitted. Be warned that the park can get very busy at weekends. Map D 1

Entry fees: Dhs.5 per person; Dhs.20 per car. Saturdays are for women and children only.

Timing: Open 08:00 to 23:00

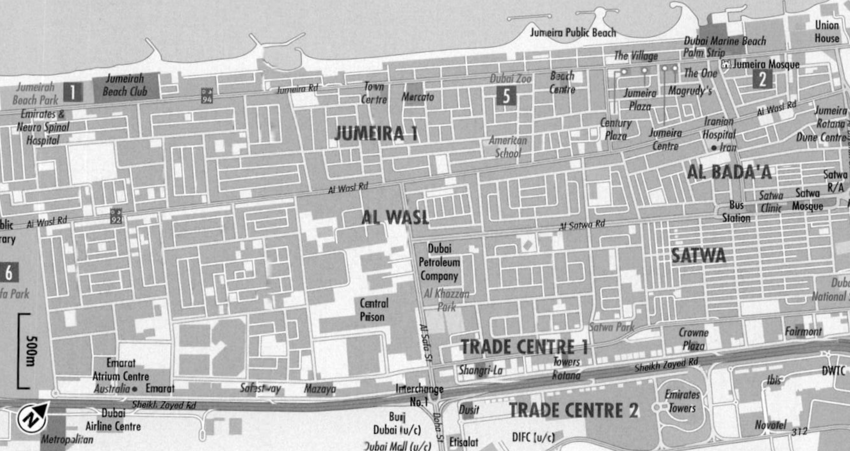

Arabian Gulf
Jumeira Public Beach
Union House
Dubai Marine Beach
Palm Strip
The Village
Jumeira Mosque
The One
2
Beach Centre
Dubai Zoo
5
Jumeira Plaza
Magrudy's
Al Wasl Rd
Jumeira Rotana
Al Diyafah St
Dune Centre
Century Plaza
Jumeira Centre
Iranian Hospital
Iran
4
AL BADA'A
Satwa R/A
Satwa Clinic
Satwa Mosque
Rydges
Bus Station
Jumeirah Beach Park
1
Jumeirah Beach Club
94
Jumeira Rd
Town Centre
Mercato
Emirates & Neuro Spinal Hospital
JUMEIRA 1
American School
Al Wasl Rd
AL WASL
Al Satwa Rd
Public Library
92
6
Safa Park
Dubai Petroleum Company
Al Khazzan Park
SATWA
Dubai National School
Central Prison
Al Safa St
Satwa Park
Crowne Plaza
Fairmont
TRADE CENTRE 1
Shangri-La
Towers Rotana
Sheikh Zayed Rd
DWTC
Ibis
500m
Emarat Atrium Centre
Australia
Emarat
Mazaya
Interchange No.1
Emirates Towers
Sheikh Zayed Rd
Dusit
TRADE CENTRE 2
Dubai Airline Centre
Burj Dubai (u/c)
Doha St
Novotel
312
2nd Za'abeel Rd
Metropolitan
Dubai Mall (u/c)
Etisalat
DIFC (u/c)
D

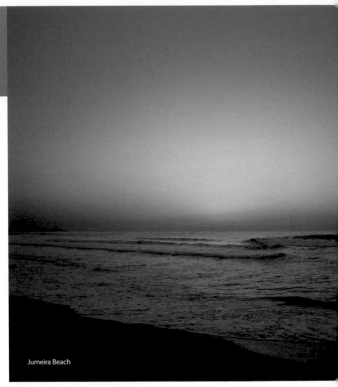

Jumeira Beach

Jumeira Mosque

04 353 6666
Jumeira Beach Road
www.cultures.ae

Located at the beginning of Beach Road, Jumeria Mosque is by far the most beautiful in the whole city, especially at night when it lights up the sky. It is also one of the very few to permit non-Muslims to enter on a tour. The Sheikh Mohammed Centre for Cultural Understanding, through its 'Open Doors, Open Minds' programme, organises guided tours on Thursday and Sunday mornings at 10:00 sharp, and it's highly recommended. Men and women are required to dress conservatively, which means no shorts and no sleeveless tops. Women are also required to cover their heads and all visitors will be asked to remove their shoes before entering. Map D 2

Majlis Ghorfat Um Al Sheef

04 394 6343
Jumeira Beach Road
www.dubaitourism.co.ae

Built in 1955 from coral stone and gypsum, this traditional Arabic house, which can be found near HSBC on Beach Road, was once used by the late Sheikh Rashid bin Saeed Al Maktoum as a summer residence. It is traditionally decorated, with an open veranda ('leewan' or 'rewaaq') on the ground floor and a 'majlis' (Arabic for 'meeting place') upstairs.

The roof terrace was once used for drying dates or by guests as a place to crash, and it once offered uninterrupted sea views – now, of course, it's surrounded by villas. Within the grounds you'll find a traditional falaj irrigation system and a barasti shelter made entirely from palm branches and leaves. Off Map

Entry fees: Dhs.1 adults: under 6 years free.

Diyafah Street

Further back from the beach towards Sheikh Zayed Road is the neighbourhood of Satwa. Busy, bohemian and a far cry from the polished preening of Jumeira, Satwa is one of the best places in the city for a late-evening stroll. The main drag is Diyafah Street, which has some great independent restaurants, including Al Mallah (p.176) and Sidra (p.180) for great shawarmas, falafel and juice.

Visit the intricate Iranian Mosque on Al Hudeiba Road (known as Plant Street), then head to the end of Diyafah Street. Nearest the sea is the Dar Al Ittehad (Union House), where the treaty to create the United Arab Emirates was signed on 2 December 1971. It is also the site of the UAE's largest flag (40mx20m), which sits atop a 120m reinforced column.

Map D 4

Dubai Zoo

04 349 6444

Jumeira Beach Road

www.dubaitourism.ae

This old-fashioned zoo began life as a private collection before being taken over by Dubai Municipality. It underwent expansion and refurbishment in the mid 1980s, but sadly hasn't seen a lick of paint since.

Lions, tigers, giraffes, monkeys, deer, snakes, bears, flamingos and giant tortoises still reside behind bars in small cages. And despite much talk of relocating to a much bigger site, it remains a somewhat squalid affair and one that animal lovers may wish to avoid. Map D 5

Entry fees: Dhs.2 per person, children under 2 are free.

Timings: The zoo is closed on Tuesdays.

Safa Park

Nr Union Co-op 04 349 2111
www.dm.gove.ae

Spot the giant ferris wheel opposite Jumeira Library and you've found the wonderfully eclectic Safa Park. In the middle of its huge expanse is a lake with a waterfall, where you can hire out rowing boats or feed the ducks. There's also plenty to entertain children, including bumper cars at weekends, a trampoline cage and a merry-go-round.

Safa's a great spot for frisbee or a kickabout, and you can also hire bikes within the park or take to the popular, sprung running track which skirts the perimeter. Tuesdays is ladies' day, but there is also a permanent ladies' garden within the park where men are not allowed at any time.

So great is Safa that there is a sequel. The ladies-only Safa Park II is a much smaller version of the original, but has the same relaxing atmosphere. Its two children's playgrounds make it popular with families.

Map D 6

Timings: Open 08:00 to 23:00

Entry fees: Dhs.3 per person; with children under three going free.

Flowered up

Who needs a supermarket florist when Satwa has a whole street dedicated to flora? Head to 'Plant Street' and choose from a huge selection of indoor and outdoor blooms, as well as garden essentials. This being Satwa, you can also pick up paint and upholstery on the same street. Just make sure you avoid the dilapidated pet shops. For more information on shopping in Satwa, see p.148.

Clockwise from top left: Jumeira Mosque, Majlis Ghorfat Um Al Sheef, Jumeirah Beach Club.

If you only do one thing in... Jumeira & Satwa

Visit the city's most beautiful mosque, and one of the few in the UAE open to non-Muslims.

Best for...

drinking and eating Start the day with a leisurely breakfast at Lime Tree Café – good coffee and great for cakes (p.179).

sightseeing As the shadows lengthen, make your way to Satwa and soak up the hustle and bustle in this underrated part of town.

shopping Enjoy a wander through the mini-malls and thriving independent shops (p.142) that line Beach Road in Jumeria.

relaxation The host of fine spas in the area are no match for a leisurely dip in the balmy Gulf waters, followed by a sundowner at Sho Cho's (p.180).

families Everywhere's a city in Dubai and this one is dedicated to Fun. Located in Mercato (p.141), Fun City is a play area jampacked with rides for kids.

New Dubai

Stunning high-rise apartments, lush golf courses and a world-class pick of bars, restaurants and spas. What else did you expect from 'new' Dubai?

Less than a decade ago, this was a simple stretch of beachfront with a sprinkling of hotels. Now it's known locally as Dubai Marina or New Dubai (officially Marsa Dubai) and is one of the most ambitious residential and leisure developments anywhere in the world. Dubai, eh?

The transformation is, and will continue to be, staggering. If you're staying in a beach-front hotel, the chances are that it's one of the many that have cropped up in double-quick time. And even if you're not staying in this part of town, it would be a huge mistake not to spend a night or two sampling 'new' Dubai in all its glory. And construction. Yep, this is where you'll find the much-hyped Palms of Jumeirah and Jebel Ali coming ashore, the futuristic and tightly packed towers of Jumeriah Beach Residence and the ridiculous opulence of the One&Only Royal Mirage and Grosvenor House hotels. And some of that infamous construction you've been reading so much about.

Although there's plenty of digging and skyscraping going on, there is still tranquility in these parts – thanks mostly to the wonderful man-made Marina, which snakes its way around the imposing towers. Once it's complete, it will house 200 high-rise buildings and cover 53 million square feet, accommodating over 120,000 people. *For **restaurants and bars** in the area, see p.182.*

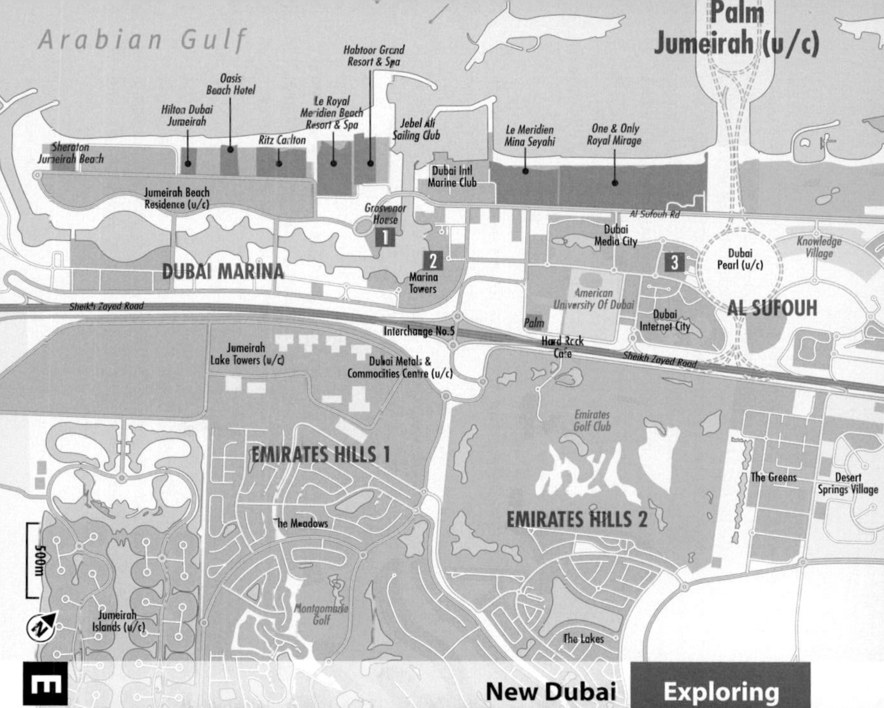
Arabian Gulf
Palm Jumeirah (u/c)
Habtoor Grand Resort & Spa
Oasis Beach Hotel
Le Royal Meridien Beach Resort & Spa
Hilton Dubai Jumeirah
Jebel Ali Sailing Club
Le Meridien Mina Seyahi
One & Only Royal Mirage
Ritz Carlton
Sheraton Jumeirah Beach
Dubai Intl Marine Club
Jumeirah Beach Residence (u/c)
Grosvenor House
1
2
3
Al Sufouh Rd
Dubai Media City
Knowledge Village
Dubai Pearl (u/c)
DUBAI MARINA
Marina Towers
American University Of Dubai
Sheikh Zayed Road
AL SUFOUH
Dubai Internet City
Palm
Interchange No.5
Hard Rock Cafe
Jumeirah Lake Towers (u/c)
Dubai Metals & Commodities Centre (u/c)
Emirates Golf Club
EMIRATES HILLS 1
The Greens
Desert Springs Village
The Meadows
EMIRATES HILLS 2
500m
Montgomerie Golf
Jumeirah Islands (u/c)
The Lakes

Grosvenor House Hotel

04 399 8888

Dubai Marina www.grosvenorhouse.lemeridien.com

Despite looking like a dumpy spaceshuttle, the Grosvenor House is one of the most sophisticated hotels in Dubai. Not content with housing the world-renowned Buddha Bar, it also boasts the rooftop Bar 44, which offers breathtaking views across the Marina and out beyond the Gulf. Among its fine restaurants is Indego, whose consultant chef Vineet Bhatia is the only Indian chef to be awarded a Michelin Star. Map E 1

Marina Walk

Dubai Marina

The area around Dubai Marina Towers was the first to be developed back in 1998 – prehistoric in Dubai terms – and is one of the most settled. It helps that it's one of the city's most desirable addresses, with close proximity to good restaurants and stunning views of the Marina and the Persian Gulf beyond.

Marina Walk, the boulevard at the base of the towers, is home to a number of independent restaurants and cafes (see Going Out, p.152), including the excellent Lebanese Chandelier and the popular Thai, Royal Orchid, as well as a supermarket, bookshop, pharmacy and a number of ATMs. It is a great place for a stroll any time but it really comes to life in the evenings and cooler months when you can sit and gaze out across the gleaming yachts and the flashing lights of high-rise hotels and apartments. On Fridays during winter it hosts the Marina Market with stalls selling clothing, jewellery, gifts and handicrafts. Map E 2

Dubai Media /Internet City/Knowledge Village

Sheikh Zayed Rd, btw interchange 4 and 5

Dubai has established a number of tax-free zones to make it easier for big multinationals to flourish in the region. Hence the thriving, self-contained Dubai Media and Internet Cities. If you happen to be driving around 'New' Dubai near the Marina during your stay, you'll see the familiar logos of CNN, Reuters and BBC World alongside local firms such as Showtime Arabia and Ten Sports. The SAS Radisson Hotel, slap bang in the middle of Media City, has a couple of decent bars should you want to mingle with newshounds. In the same area you'll also find Knowledge Village, Dubai's oversized collection of schools and colleges. Map E 3

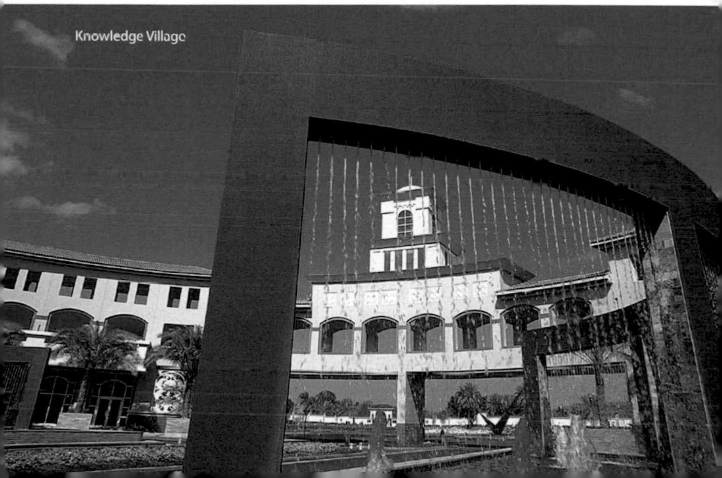
Knowledge Village

Clockwise from top left:
One&Only Royal Mirage, Jumeira Beach, Dubai Marina

If you only do one thing in...
New Dubai

Grab a table at one of Marina Walk's restaurants and watch the world and its yachts go by.

Best for...

drinking and eating A dead-heat between Buddha Bar and Bar 44. The choice is yours at the Grosvenor House Hotel. (p.237).

sightseeing The view across the Arabian Gulf from Bar 44 (p.184) is sensational, as is its drinks menu and cute canapes.

shopping On a Friday between October and April head for the bustling art and crafts market on the edge of the Marina.

relaxation 'New' Dubai is blessed with numerous five-star hotels offering fantastic spas and treatments.

families Treat the kids to a guided tour of Ibn Battuta (p.139) shopping mall, then let them loose on the fountain at Marina Walk.

Oud Metha & Umm Hurair

Small in size, but not in stature, this central spot stays in the memory for two very good reasons...

Slap bang in the middle of Dubai you'll find one of its more curious, smaller districts. But what it lacks in size and obvious character, it makes up for in shopping and great, big leisure parks. Go-karting, anyone? *For **restaurants and bars** in the area, see p.190.*

Wafi City

Umm Hurair
04 324 0000
www.waficity.com

The area's landmark development is Wafi City, a self-contained retail and leisure complex. Before you start your shopping spree in its vast walkways, take time out to look at the two stained glass pyramid roofs. Now you've picked up the Egyptian theme, it's time to explore Wafi Mall (p.153).

It's stuffed with designer boutiques selling the latest couture, jewellery and accessories, and the Pyramids, which includes Pharoah's Leisure Club, Cleopatra's Spa and a number of restaurants including Asha's (p.190) and Medzo (p.194). The mall has any number of futuristically named zones, the best one being Galactica. Here you can take on teenagers at inline skating (skateboarding if you must). Lunarland and Encounter Zones are really for kids, however much you fancy the soft-play area. The already impressive site is being further developed to include the striking Raffles Dubai Hotel and Khan Murjan – a subterranean souk for artists. Map F 1

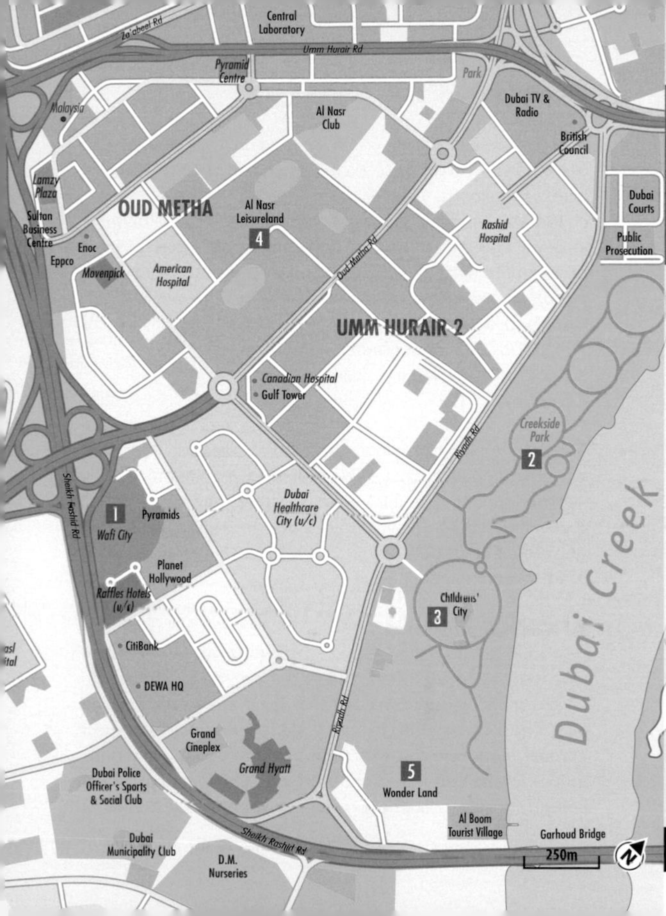

F

OUD METHA
UMM HURAIR 2

Za'abeel Rd
Central Laboratory
Umm Hurair Rd
Pyramid Centre
Park
Al Nasr Club
Dubai TV & Radio
British Council
Dubai Courts
Public Prosecution
Malaysia
Lamzy Plaza
Sultan Business Centre
Enoc
Eppco
Movenpick
American Hospital
Al Nasr Leisureland
4
Oud Metha Rd
Rashid Hospital
Canadian Hospital
Gulf Tower
Creekside Park
2
Riyadh Rd
Sheikh Rashid Rd
1
Pyramids
Wafi City
Dubai Healthcare City (u/c)
Planet Hollywood
Raffles Hotels (u/c)
Childrens' City
3
Dubai Creek
CitiBank
DEWA HQ
Grand Cineplex
Grand Hyatt
Riyadh Rd
5
Wonder Land
Dubai Police Officer's Sports & Social Club
Al Boom Tourist Village
Garhoud Bridge
250m
N
Dubai Municipality Club
Sheikh Rashid Rd
D.M. Nurseries
asl
ital

Creekside Park

Nr Wonderland — 04 336 7633 — www.dm.gov.ae

There is serious relaxation to be had in Oud Metha. And Creekside Park is where to do it. With 2.5km of creek frontage, acres of gardens, fishing piers, jogging tracks, BBQ sites, children's play areas, restaurants and kiosks – it's the ultimate in Dubai park life. To remind yourself that you're in the fastest growing city in the world, take the park's cable car which allows visitors an unrestricted view of Dubai from 30 metres in the air. Once back on the ground, grab a four-wheel bike, available for hire for Dhs.20 per hour from gate two. Map F 2

Children's City

Creekside Park — 04 334 0808 — www.childrencity.com

The scary looking blue building within Creekside Park is an educational project that offers kids their own learning zone (themed around the solar system, natural environment and the human body). The main activities are aimed at children between 5 and 12 years old but there's enough to keep toddlers entertained. Map F 3

Al Nasr Leisureland

Behind American Hospital — 04 337 1234 — www.alnasrleisureland.ae

Opened way back in 1979, this is the nearest Dubai gets to an old-school leisure park. With an ice-skating rink, bowling alley and arcade games it's every teenager's dream and most parents' nightmare. But with tennis courts, a gym and regular indoor football, there's no doubt that Al Nasr is a great facility. Should your stay coincide with your child's birthday, the Fruit &

Garden Luna Park with its bumper cars and mini rollercoaster is a neat little place for a party. Map F 4

Wonderland Theme & Water Park

04 324 1222

Nr Creekside Park

www.wonderlanduae.com

Dubailand (see p.26) may be lurking in the distance, but for now Wonderland remains Dubai's only theme park, and much-loved it is too. Combining an amusements and water park, Wonderland will keep even the most distracted teenager in check with trampolines, video games and go-karting. For any adults who should know better, there's paintballing. Map F 5

Wafi Pyramids

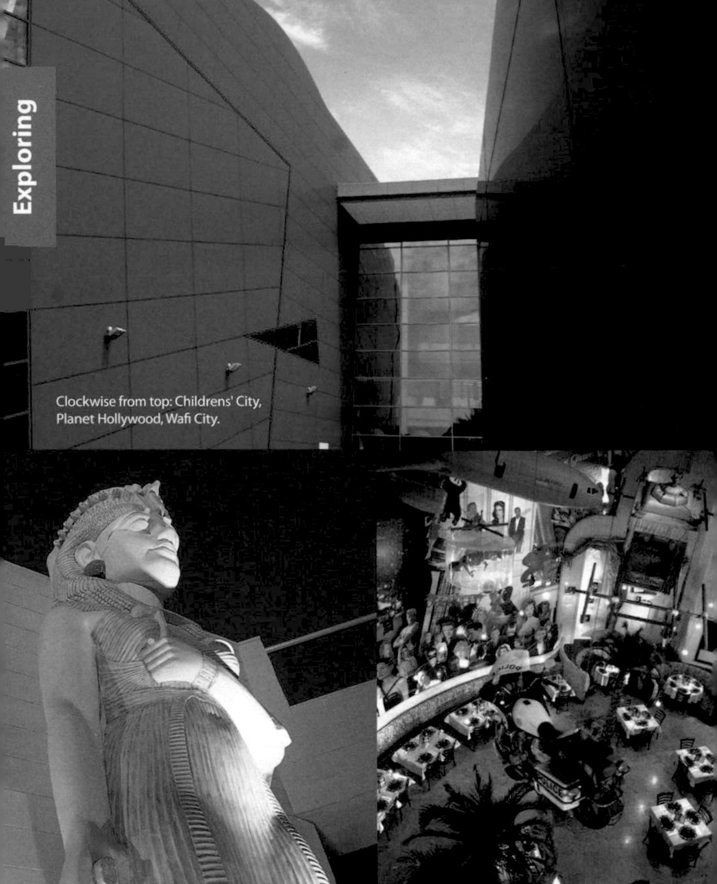

Clockwise from top: Childrens' City, Planet Hollywood, Wafi City.

If you only do one thing in...

Oud Metha & Umm Hurair

Sample the joys of shopping, spas and oversized cocktails – all under one roof at Wafi City.

Best for...

drinking and eating The Pyramids has a few excellent restaurants, but it's the modern Indian delights of Asha's that capture the imagination (p.190).

sightseeing Squeeze yourself into one of the cable cars that runs the length of Creekside Park. The best view of the city without hiring a chopper.

shopping With over 200 shops selling over 1,000 fashion brands, Wafi Mall (p.72) is designer decadence.

relaxation Dubai park life doesn't get any better than at Creekside, especially if you've got kids in tow.

families Your little ones are spoilt for choice in this area, but to keep them occupied all afternoon head to Children's City within Creekside Park.

Sheikh Zayed Road

'New' Dubai may have caught the eye with its modern luxury, but the heart remains in Sheikh Zayed – still the most exciting strip in all Dubai.

During the day, this impressive, densely populated 3.5km stretch of road offers unrivalled views of Dubai from some of the most striking buildings in this or any city. At night, it buzzes with people shuffling from one bar to the next and back again. Dubai's most important thoroughfare is named after the hugely popular former President of the UAE who died in 1994, so it's fitting that it's become so much more than the main route from Dubai to Abu Dhabi. Straight roads don't come much more iconic.

Thanks to a concentration of top hotels, you've got the pick of limitless dining and entertainment options. Some of Dubai's favourite bars, restaurants and clubs are along this strip, including Spectrum on One in the Fairmont, Teatro (p.202) and Long's Bar in the Towers Rotana and Trader Vic's in the Crowne Plaza (p.202). Arabica and Zyara are also good cafes for local food and shisha and Saj Express is known for its cheap Arabic food. There are also enough coffee shops and cafes to satisfy the most ardent caffeine junky. The five-star hotels on Sheikh Zayed Road also make it one of the city's top destinations for pampering. From the Willow Stream Spa at the Fairmont Hotel (p.129), to The Health Club & Spa at Shangri-La, and the men only 1847

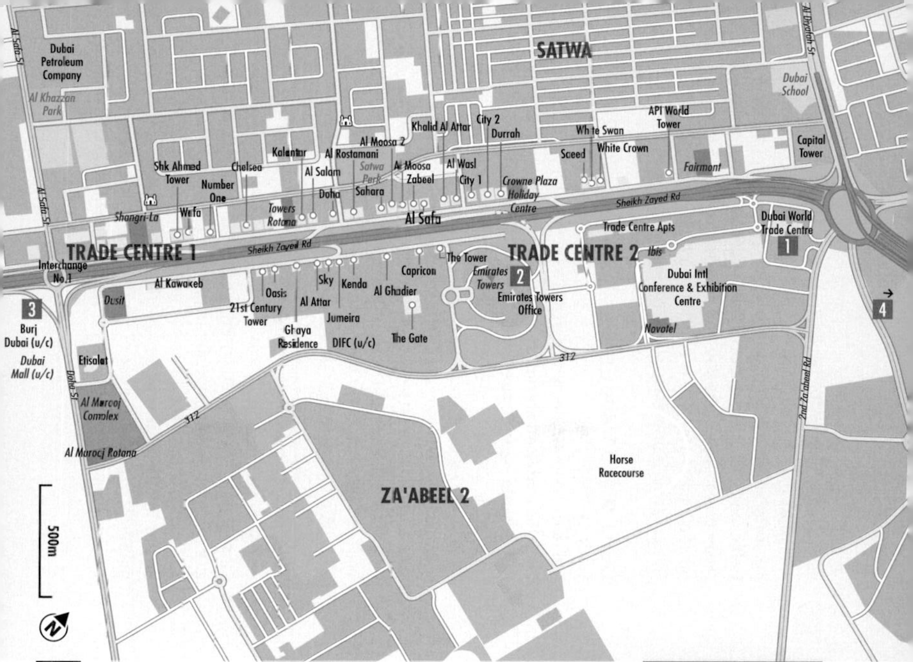

SATWA
Dubai Petroleum Company
Al Khazzan Park
Al Safa St
Dubai School
Al Diyafah St
API World Tower
Capital Tower
City 2
Durrah
Khalid Al Attar
White Swan
White Crown
Sceed
Fairmont
Al Moosa 2
Al Rostamani
Kalantar
Al Salam
Satwa Park
Al Moosa
Zabeel
Al Wasl
City 1
Crowne Plaza
Holiday Centre
Shk Ahmed Tower
Chelsea
Number One
Doha
Sahara
Wafa
Shangri-La
Towers Rotana
Al Safa
Sheikh Zayed Rd
Trade Centre Apts
Dubai World Trade Centre
1
TRADE CENTRE 1
TRADE CENTRE 2
Ibis
Interchange No.1
Al Kawakeb
Oasis
21st Century Tower
Sky
Kenda
Al Attar
Jumeira
Ghaya Residence
DIFC (u/c)
Al Ghadier
Capricon
The Tower
The Gate
Emirates Towers
2
Emirates Towers Office
Dubai Intl Conference & Exhibition Centre
Novotel
4
3
Burj Dubai (u/c)
Dubai Mall (u/c)
Dusit
Etisalat
Doha St
Al Murooj Complex
Al Murooj Rotana
312
2nd Za'abeel Rd
Horse Racecourse
ZA'ABEEL 2
500m
N

G

at Emirates Towers Boulevard, there's a treatment to suit everyone. The only bad point of this buzzing part of town is, ironically, Sheikh Zayed Road itself. The combination of heavy traffic and the lack of pedestrian subways or over-passes mean that it could take you half an hour to reach a building on the other side of the road. Still, it'll be worth the wait. *For **restaurants and bars** in the area, see p.196.*

Dubai World Trade Centre

04 332 1000
Trade Centre 2
www.dwtc.com

Flanked on either side by impressive towers and skyscrapers, Sheikh Zayed Road's business district starts at the landmark Dubai World Trade Centre and exhibition halls (illustrated on the Dhs.100 banknote). When it was completed in the 1970s, the 39-storey tower was by far the tallest building in Dubai and it paved the way for the city's great skyscraper revolution. For a great view, especially in winter when it is less hazy, try the guided tour to the observation deck (09:30 and 16:30 everyday except Fridays; tours leave from the lobby information desk and cost Dhs.10). Map G 1

Emirates Towers

04 330 0000
Trade Centre 2
www.jumeirah.com

Close by and looking down on most other buildings in the city (but not for long), are the impressive Emirates Towers. At 355 metres, the Office Tower is currently the tallest building in the Middle East and Europe. The smaller tower, at 305 metres, houses the Emirates Towers five-star hotel. The views across downtown Dubai from the aptly named 51st floor cocktail bar, Vu's, are superb. Boulevard, also at Emirates Towers (p.144), is Dubai's most exclusive mall and home to a selection of designer clothes outlets, jewellery and perfume shops. Most of the towers which line Sheikh Zayed Road also have small shops on the ground floor where you can pick up the essentials. Map G 2

Burj Dubai

Sheikh Zayed Rd, interchange 1 www.burjdubai.com

A little further down Sheikh Zayed Road beyond the first interchange is what the city claims to be the 'most prestigious square kilometre on the planet'. This being Dubai, that statement is not without substance. Well under way in the centre of the development is the Burj Dubai.

Aiming to be the world's tallest building, at around 700 metres, it should be completed by the end of 2008. If that's a bit high and mighty for you, there's always the Thunderbowl on the other side of the highway. Who cares about breaking records when there's ten-pin bowling to be played. Map G 3

Za'abeel Park

Nr Trade Centre R/A

Next to Trade Centre Roundabout you'll find Dubai's newest expanse of greenery. It covers a whopping 52 hectares and includes recreational areas for children and adults, a jogging track and cricket pitch. Oh, and an IMAX cinema no less. It's also the first park in the Middle East with a 'technology theme' and features three zones for the kids to learn things: alternative energy, communications and technology. Map G 4

Clockwise from top left: Fairmont Hotel, Dusit Dubai Hotel, Emirates Towers.

If you only do one thing on...
Sheikh Zayed Road

Get a bird's-eye view of downtown Dubai from the observation desk at the top of the World Trade Centre.

Best for...

drinking and eating Head for Long's Bar at the Towers Rotana – home to Dubai's finest happy hours.

sightseeing Before it gets too dark, take the lift to the 51st floor of the Emirates Towers. The view from cocktail bar, Vu's (p.202), is unforgettable.

shopping Treat yourself at Boulevard in Emirates Towers (p.144), packed with Dubai's most exclusive designer boutiques.

relaxation The Willow Stream Spa (p.127) at the dramatic Fairmont Hotel is heaven on earth, and The Health Club at Shangri-La is a close second.

families Unleash the competitive dad and mum in you with a game of ten-pin bowling at the true bowlers' choice, Thunderbowl.

Umm Suqeim

Don't let rows and rows of residential housing fool you. Umm Suqeim plays host to not one but two of the world's most iconic attractions.

If you like water parks and world famous hotels, then you're going to love Umm Suqeim. For the most part, it's a pleasant family neighbourhood, unlikely to make most traveller's itineraries save for a hotel in the shape of a mighty, billowing sail. *For **restaurants and bars** in the area, see p.204.*

Burj Al Arab

04 301 7777
Umm Suqeim
www.burj-al-arab.com

Currently the world's tallest hotel, the Burj Al Arab is also one of the most-photographed residences in the world, helped largely by Tiger Woods teeing off from its helipad over 1,000 feet up. Nestled 280m off the coast on its own island, the Burj's billowing-sail design is as striking a structure as you'll see anywhere in the world. And inside it's no less spectacular. If your budget allows, you shouldn't miss the opportunity to sample what sensational luxury feels like in one of the bars, restaurants and spas, or at least enjoy afternoon tea at Sahn Eddar. Impressive whichever way you look at it. Map H 1

Souk Madinat

04 366 8888
Umm Suqeim
www.jumeirah.com

Although not nearly as tall, the area's other luxury hotels are no less impressive, and each have a number of great restaurants

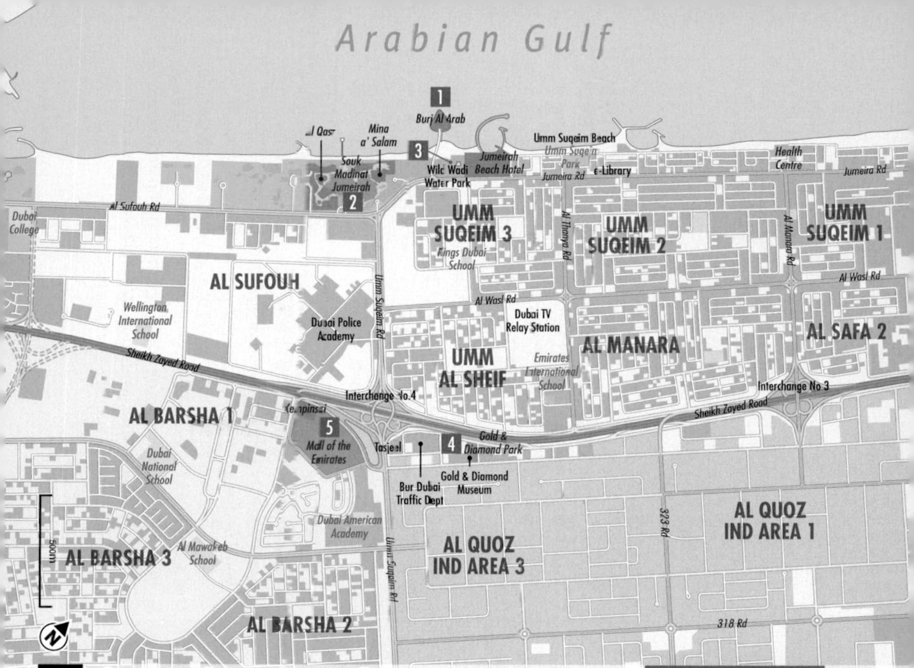

Arabian Gulf

1 Burj Al Arab
2 Souk Madinat Jumeirah
3 Wild Wadi Water Park
4 Gold & Diamond Park
5 Mall of the Emirates

Al Qasr
Mina a' Salam
Jumeirah Beach Hotel
Umm Suqeim Beach
Umm Suqeim Park
e-Library
Health Centre
Jumeira Rd
Al Sufouh Rd
Dubai College
UMM SUQEIM 3
Kings Dubai School
Al Thanya Rd
UMM SUQEIM 2
Al Manara Rd
UMM SUQEIM 1
Al Wasl Rd
AL SUFOUH
Wellington International School
Dubai Police Academy
Umm Suqeim Rd
Dubai TV Relay Station
AL MANARA
AL SAFA 2
UMM AL SHEIF
Emirates International School
Sheikh Zayed Road
Interchange No.4
Interchange No 3
Kempinski
AL BARSHA 1
Tasjeel
Bur Dubai Traffic Dept
Gold & Diamond Museum
Dubai National School
Dubai American Academy
323 Rd
AL QUOZ IND AREA 1
AL QUOZ IND AREA 3
AL BARSHA 3
Al Mawakeb School
500m
AL BARSHA 2
318 Rd
N

H

and bars. The Souk Madinat Jumeirah is located just a stone's throw from the Burj Al Arab, (see Shopping p.152). Built to resemble a traditional Arabian market, the souk is a maze of alleyways featuring 75 open-fronted shops and boutiques. For weary shoppers, there are numerous coffee shops, restaurants and bars. Map H 2

Wild Wadi

04 348 4444
Next to Burj Al Arab
www.wildwadi.com

Spread over 12 acres beside the Jumeirah Beach Hotel, Wild Wadi Water Park has 30 aquatic rides and attractions to suit all ages and levels of bravado.

From the recently opened Juha's Dhow & Lagoon aimed at the park's youngest visitors, to the Jumeirah Sceirah – the tallest and fastest freefall water slide outside North America – there's something for you and your more adventurous alter-ego. Map H 3

Gold & Diamond Park

04 347 7788
Nr Dubai Police College
www.goldanddiamondpark.com

It's logical that the world's leading re-exporter of gold has a whole park dedicated to bling. Centrally located on junction four of Sheikh Zayed Road, it has most of the shops you'd find in the main malls but in a much calmer setting. If you've finally decided to take the plunge with a wedding or engagement ring you'd be well advised to spend a few hours here. As with outlets in the souks, you can commission pieces. There's also a French Connection cafe while you reflect on that big decision. Map H 4

Ski Dubai

04 409 4000

Al Barsha

www.skidxb.com

Never mind the shopping at Mall of the Emirates, how's the powder looking? Yep, here it is, the Middle East's first indoor ski slope, complete with black run, half-pipe, chair lifts and annoyingly cool instructors. As you get the escalator down from Starbucks, you'll think Ski Dubai is some elaborate joke such is its incongruous location slap bang in the middle of the Mall. But once you've slipped on the salopettes and had your first face-full of snow, you'll realise that this is deadly serious, and your turning technique is still all wrong. Map 5

Burj Al Arab

Clockwise from top left: Rooftop Lounge at Royal Mirage, Al Muntaha, Souk Madinat Jumeirah.

If you only do one thing in...

Umm Suqeim

Beg, borrow or suffer horrendous debt. Sell your house. Just make sure you sample a drink, dinner or stay a night at the Burj Al Arab.

Best for...

drinking and eating An evening at the Souk Madinat Jumeirah will always be special, and a terrace table at Shoo Fee Ma Fee (p.211) is something else.

sightseeing Atop Wild Wadi's *Jumeirah Sceirah*, the largest and fastest freefall water ride outside of North America, you'll get an extraordinary view of the Burj.

shopping And skiing and five-star luxury... it's Mall of the Emirates (p.140) in all its overstated glory.

relaxation How about your own bungalow amid the landscaped grounds of the Six Senses Spa (p.125) within Souk Madinat.

families Summit Surge and Rushdown Ravine – 170 metres of the premier family ride at Wild Wadi.

Further out

Arabian Ranches (Global Village)

It might sound like something out of an 80s TV series, but Arabian Ranches is actually one of Dubai's most luxurious villa-only developments. As well lush greenery, lakes and the Desert Course golf course, you'll also find the Global Village in its midst. Initially opened for just two months of the year, this 'cultural entertainment centre' is a smorgasbord of music, dance, arts and theatre (all from different countries, see?). There are various pavilions where you can see a motley collection of craftsmen producing everything from an intricately woven Indian shawl to a Japanese bonsai tree. Global Village is part of Dubailand. Currently under development, Dubailand will be the biggest theme park in the world when it's completed. Eventually it will cover a staggering two billion square feet, making it twice the size of Disneyland.

Hatta

Nestled at the foot of the Hajar Mountains, Hatta is a small town about 100km from Dubai city and 10km from the Dubai/Oman border. Home to the oldest fort in the emirate, which was built in 1790, Hatta is a tranquil change of scene. You'll find the excellent Hatta Fort Hotel (04 852 3211) should you just want to unwind, and the recreation of a traditional mountain village if you're looking for a glimpse of the past. But head out of the village and into the mountains and the picture changes dramatically thanks to the Hatta Pools – deep, strangely shaped canyons that have been carved out by rushing floodwater. Later in the afternoon, as you head back towards Dubai, you'll come across another of the UAE's obsessions as tranquility disappears, and huge 4WDs and quad bikes roar up and down the side of 'Big Red', the area's most famous sand dune.

Jebel Ali

Back in the day Jebel Ali was something of an outpost, stuck south-west of Dubai on the long road to Abu Dhabi. But the development of Dubai Marina soon put a stop to that. Now much closer to the action, Jebel Ali retains a rare old-school charm. One of the main draws is Jebel Ali Golf Resort and Spa (p.239) with its nine-hole course (routinely invaded by peacocks, bizarrely), private beach, marina and spa. Nearby, you'll also find the Jebel Ali Shooting Club, with five floodlit clay shooting ranges for skeet, trap and sport shooting. Non-members are welcome, and there are professional instructors on hand to give lessons in archery and shooting.

Nad Al Sheba

Home to the world's richest horserace, the Dubai World Cup, Nad Al Sheba also boasts a premier golf course and regularly holds camel racing on its desert track. Horse-racing fans should head for its breakfast stable tour which offers a behind-the-scenes glimpse of the jockey's facilities, plus the chance to see horses in training. The tour ends at the Godolphin Gallery, an exhibition charting the success of the Maktoum family's private racing stable. Not far from Nad Al Sheba is Ras Al Khor Wildlife Sanctuary and its collection of flamingos and waders. On an average day in winter there are up to 15,000 birds under Dubai Municipality protection.

Tours and safaris

Guided tours are a quick and easy way to see more of the UAE – whether you want to take to water or camp deep in the desert.

Tours – Dubai

Bus Tours

Depending on how hot it is, you can jump on and off one of the eight open-top London double deckers that roam Dubai's streets. They board at Wafi City and Deira City Centre. Call 04 324 4187 for more information. The amphibious Wonder Bus takes passengers on a two hour mini tour of Dubai. Concentrating on the creek, it also covers Creekside Park and Dubai Creek Golf Club, and dips into the water under Maktoum Bridge towards Garhoud Bridge, then up the boat ramp and back to BurJuman. Call 04 359 5656 for more information.

Dubai City Tour

This is a half-day overview of old and new Dubai. Sights include souks, the fish market, mosques, abras, Bastakiya windtower houses and the striking buildings of the commercial sector.

Dubai by Night

This early evening tour takes in the palaces, mosques and souks of the city. It's a good opportunity to soak up the city before enjoying dinner at one of the city's restaurants.

Mosque Tours

Non-Muslims are not usually allowed into mosques but the Sheikh Mohammed Centre for Cultural Understanding organises tours around the impressive Jumeira mosque. Tours can also been booked through operators and start at 10:00 sharp on Sunday and Thursday mornings.

Shopping Tour

From designer clothes, shoes and jewellery in the malls to electronics, spices and textiles in the souks, everything is available in Dubai. This half-day tour takes in some of the hottest shopping spots, including the main malls and shopping districts such as Karama, giving you plenty of scope to practise your bargaining skills.

Tours and safaris – out of Dubai

Desert Safaris

Experience a rollercoaster ride across the dunes and try your hand at sandskiing, before enjoying the sunset and a barbecue at a permanent Bedouin-style camp, followed by shisha, belly dancing and henna painting.

For the dune dinners, the tours leave around 16:00, passing through great scenery before a spot of dune bashing and dinner at a Bedouin campsite. Tours usually head back to Dubai around 22:00. On the overnight safari, you'll start at around 15:00 with a drive through the dunes to a Bedouin-style campsite, dine under the stars, and sleep in the fresh air.

Hatta Pools Safari

This full-day tour takes in the remarkable Hatta Pools in the Hajar Mountains, and usually includes a stop at the Hatta Fort Hotel.

Full-Day Safari

If desert is your thing, this is the tour for you; it passes through traditional Bedouin villages and camel farms, surrounded by huge red sand dunes. Most tours also visit Fossil Rock and the Hajar Mountains.

Mountain Safaris

Taking in some of the most outstanding scenery in the country, you'll head north to Ras Al Khaimah before travelling through the Hajar Mountains at Wadi Bih, passing terraced mountainsides and stone houses, at over 1,200 metres above sea level. You'll leave the mountains at Dibba and return on the highway. Some full-day tours start at Dibba.

Abu Dhabi Tour

You'll visit the Women's Handicraft Centre, the Heritage Village, the Petroleum Exhibition and Abu Dhabi's most famous landmark, the corniche, on this full-day tour of the UAE's capital.

Liwa Tour

The Liwa Oasis is an amazing place where life clings to a small pocket of greenery in one of the most barren areas on earth. Check overpage for operators who offer this tour.

Ajman & Sharjah Tour

Great for anyone interested in the UAE's past. Visit the working dhow yards in Ajman before exploring the famous museums and souks of Sharjah (Half day).

Al Ain Tour

From the 4,000 year-old tombs at Hili to the 175 year-old Al Nahyan family fort and the UAE's only remaining camel market, Al Ain has plenty to recommend a tour.

Ras Al Khaimah Tour

Travel up the 'pirate coast' to the oldest seaport in the region to check out Ras Al Khaimah museum and old town, before returning through the stunningly beautiful Hajar Mountains.

East Coast Tour

This tour takes in the spectacular East Coast scenery, the oldest mosque in the Emirates and usually a visit to the Friday Market (open all week). The tour lasts all day.

Tour operators

There are a number of operators who organise tours in and out of Dubai. Your hotel or concierge will be happy to book a specific tour. If not, here is a pick of the operators who offer a wide range of tours.

Arabian Adventures
04 303 4888

Desert Rangers
04 340 2408

Dubai Travel and Tourist Services
04 336 7727

Net Tours
04 266 8661

Off-Road Adventures
04 343 2288

Other emirates

Had your fill of modern luxury? Then head to the UAE's other emirates and appreciate this country's phenomenal natural beauty.

Abu Dhabi

Dubai is often mistaken as the capital of the UAE thanks to the 'Sydney Syndrome'. In fact, it's further south where you'll find the true king of the desert and capital, Abu Dhabi. Oil was discovered here in 1958 and today it accounts for 10% of the world's known crude oil reserves. No wonder, then, that it's home to numerous internationally renowned hotels, including the world's most expensive hotel, Emirates Palace.

The city itself lies on an island shaped liked a scorpion and is connected to the mainland by a causeway, and is home to a selection of shiny shopping malls and a sprinkling of culture in the form of heritage and cultural sites and souks. It's acquired a growing reputation, with many visitors preferring its slightly slower pace and slightly cheaper prices than Dubai. In the cooler months the newly renovated and extended corniche is a lovely spot for a stroll.

Al Ain

Al Ain straddles the border with the Sultanate of Oman; the UAE side is known as Al Ain and the Oman side as Buraimi. Lying 148km east of Abu Dhabi city, it forms part of the Buraimi Oasis. In the days before the oil boom, it took a five-day camel

Clockwise from top left: Sharjah Corniche, Snoopy Island, Fujairah, Emirates Palace Hotel.

trek to reach the city from Abu Dhabi. Today, it will take you about an hour and a half along a gleaming highway (just watch the speed bumps as you enter town). There is evidence of the area having been inhabited for at least the last 4,000 years and the city's unique archaeological heritage and historic identity make it a recommended destination during your stay in Dubai. Among the highlights are the UAE's last camel market, where you can catch the traders bartering for their prized 'ships of the desert'. It's only open in the mornings, so you'll have time to explore the museum on the edge of the main Al Ain Oasis. The museum has an interesting collection of photographs along with Bedouin jewellery, musical instruments, and a reconstruction of a traditional majlis.

Liwa

A couple of hours south of Abu Dhabi by car lies the Liwa Oasis, which is situated on the edge of the imposing Rub Al Khali desert (also known as the Empty Quarter). If you're looking for spectacular scenery and enjoy a spot of camping, a trip into the dunes here is possibly one of the most rewarding experiences in the country. The scale is hard to describe, but imagine standing at the top of a 300 metre-high dune (if you get that far) and looking out over a 'sea' of sand that stretches to the horizon in every direction. It's desolate and remote, but quite breathtaking and thoroughly recommended. The driving is hard and should only be attempted by experienced off-roaders, in groups, with all the necessary equipment. If you're not up to the challenge, some of the tour companies listed on p.95 organise trips.

Ajman

It may be the smallest of the seven emirates, but Ajman's attractions are growing by the day. If you want a short trip out of Dubai, you could do worse than investigate one of the largest dhow building centres in the region. It's a great chance to see these massive wooden boats – the lifeline of Dubai's creek – being built with such rudimentary tools.

The old souk too, is another traditional reminder of a slower pace of life. This quiet emirate also has some great beaches and a pleasant corniche, and if you plan an overnight stay, the Ajman Kempinski Hotel & Resort (06 745 1555) provides excellent accommodation.

Umm Al Quwain

Despite plans to build 9,000 homes and a marina in this, the second smallest of the emirates, it remains a relatively quiet area, best known for a huge variety of activities for enthusiastic outdoor types. It is home to flying clubs, shooting clubs and car racing clubs, while the sheltered waters of its large lagoon are popular for watersports, and its mangroves a haven for local wildlife. One of the emirate's most popular attractions is Dreamland Aqua Park (06 768 1888, www.dreamlanduae.com), one of the largest water parks in the world. With water rides for all the family, a go-kart track and a variety of cafes, restaurants and a licensed pool bar, there's plenty to tempt families to make the trip. And if all that action leaves you too tired to think about heading back to Dubai, you can camp overnight at the park.

Ras Al Khaimah

With the majestic Hajar Mountains rising just behind the city, and the Arabian Gulf stretching out from the shore, Ras Al Khaimah (RAK) has possibly the best scenery of any emirate in the UAE. The most northerly of the seven emirates, RAK is less than an hour's drive from Dubai on the Emirates Road.

If you're visiting for the day you should make time to visit the souk in the old town and the National Museum of Ras Al Khaimah. As well as displays of jewellery and local archaeological finds, it has an account of the British naval expedition against RAK, in 1809.

RAK is the starting or finishing point for a spectacular trip through the mountains via Wadi Bih to Dibba on the East Coast and is also the entry point to the Mussandam Peninsula in Oman, and the ancient sites of Ghalilah and Shimal. Also worth quick stops are the hot springs at Khatt and the camel racetrack at Digdagga.

Sharjah

Like Dubai, Sharjah grew inland from an original creekside town, and its creek is still a prominent landmark. Sharjah is probably best known for its souks and museums. The Central Souk (aka the Blue Souk) shouldn't be missed. The souk is intricately decorated and based on Islamic design. The buildings are covered and air conditioned, with one side selling a range of gifts, knick-knacks, furniture, carved wood and souvenirs, and the other dominated by jewellery stores. There are over 600 shops, with outlets on the upper level selling an amazing range of carpets. Bargaining is expected so practise downstairs on something small before heading upstairs for that prize rug. Part of the Heritage Area, Souk Al Arsah is probably the oldest souk in Sharjah. It has been renovated in recent years, so although it has retained the feel of the old market place, it's now covered and air conditioned. The Heritage Area itself has been beautifully and sympathetically restored and includes a number of notable buildings including Al Hisn Fort (Sharjah Fort); Sharjah Islamic Museum; and Sharjah Heritage Museum (Bait Al Naboodah).

East Coast

Rugged mountains, beautiful sandy beaches and some of the region's best diving and snorkeling make a trip to the east coast highly recommended, however long you plan to stay in the UAE. You can get to the coast from Dubai in under two hours, with the drive taking you through the rugged Hajar Mountains. Whether you want to camp, hit the dunes in a 4WD or go scuba diving, there's plenty to keep you occupied.

At the foot of the Hajar Mountains, halfway down the east coast between Dibba and Fujairah is Khor Fakkan. This charming town is a favourite place for weekend breaks thanks to its attractive waterfront and beach and its setting in a bay, flanked on either side by two headlands, (hence its alternative name 'Creek of the Two Jars').

Fujairah

Fujairah, the youngest of the seven emirates, is the only city on the east coast and makes an excellent base to explore the countryside and discover wadis, forts, waterfalls and natural hot springs. The fort overlooking the town is around 300 years old and is just one of many in the city and surrounding hills, which lend the area a distinct charm. The area between the Hilton Hotel and Khor Kalba still hosts the traditional sport of 'bull butting' on Friday afternoons during the winter. The sport consists of two huge bulls going head-to-head for several rounds. It's not as cruel or barbaric as other forms of bull fighting but animal lovers may still want to shy away. The mountain village of Bithna, on the road from Fujairah to Sharjah, is best known for its fort and archaeological site. The fort once controlled the main pass through the mountains and is still impressive. The archaeological site is thought to have been a communal burial site dating from 1,350 and 300BC, and you'll find a detailed display of the tomb in Fujairah Museum.

Sultanate of Oman

After a long week in the malls of Dubai, you have the perfect antidote just a few hours away by car or plane. The Sultanate of Oman is a peaceful, breathtakingly beautiful place with enough history and heritage to keep you occupied long after the weekend. The capital Muscat has been carefully redeveloped in recent times, but it's still embedded in traditional culture. This is a very proud and friendly city, protective of its past, hence the lush greenery, stunning beaches and pristine streets. Nestled between the sea and a protective circle of hills, and neighboured by Al Qurm, Ruwi and the old town, is Mutrah. Epitomising Oman's efforts at beautification, Mutrah Corniche shows how far Oman has come since the early 1970s. The Corniche runs for about three kilometres along the Mutrah harbour, and is lined with pristine gardens and waterfalls. At its northern end, the old traders' houses and the Lawati Mosque showcase traditional architecture, with windtowers designed to capture the slightest cooling breeze. Mutrah is also famous for its souk. Considered by many to be the best in the Gulf, it's a haven for bargain hunters, explorers and history lovers alike.

Mussandam

If time allows, the Mussandam peninsula to the north-west is highly recommended, with its main cities of Khasab and Bukha, and with completely different scenery from the rest of Oman. It is sometimes called the 'Norway of the Middle East', since the jagged mountain cliffs plunge directly into the sea and the coastline is littered with inlets and fjords. Just metres off the shore are beautiful coral beds with an amazing variety of sea life, including tropical fish, turtles, dolphins, occasionally sharks, and even whales on the eastern side, making this one of the best dive sites in the Middle East. A dhow trip into the fjords is a great way to sample the beauty of Mussandam. On a full-day trip you'll see isolated coastal villages, get a chance to swim and snorkel in the calm waters, and hopefully see dolphins frolicking beside your boat. The southern province of Dhofar, and its capital Salalah, provide a welcome change in climate in the hot summer months. The monsoon (khareef) blowing in off the Indian Ocean ensures a high percentage of rainfall , resulting in cool weather and beautiful greenery.

For further reading, see ***Abu Dhabi mini Explorer, Oman Explorer***, ***UAE Off-Road Explorer***, ***Oman Off-Road Explorer***.

Sports & Spas

Sports and activities

It's not all shopping, spas and the sedentary life – Dubai takes its sport very seriously, too.

It might be the home of self-indulgent pleasures, but Dubai is also the proud host of some of the world's biggest sporting events – which means you get a rare chance to see famous faces up close without the usual cost and mayhem of many international events.

If that all sounds a little sedentary, there's plenty of scope to unleash your competitive streak. Whether you want to hack your way around one of the world's best golf courses, waterski off the west coast or play your mum at ping pong, Dubai will soon have you sweating out your holiday excess.

Among the most laidback of the big events is the Dubai Desert Classic Golf Championship, held each January at Emirates Golf Club, where Ernie Els, Tiger Woods and Colin Montgomerie work their magic on the incongruous green fairways. In February, the Dubai Tennis Championships draws the crowds, as Roger Federer and Rafael Nadal renew their rivalry in front of packed crowds at the Dubai Tennis Stadium in the Aviation Club (see p.52). Should you feel like fine-tuning your backhand, there are eight outdoor courts here, and numerous floodlit courts at various health and beach clubs. There are also air-conditioned indoor courts for hire at

Sports & Spas

Insportz (04 347 5833), where you can also play a spot of cricket or indoor football.

It's little surprise that Dubai is also home to the world's richest horse race, the illustrious World Cup. If you happen to be in town in March, don't miss this opportunity to see the city's great and good coming out to play. The venue, Nad Al Sheba Club, is an internationally renowned racing facility and its floodlit meetings, held from November through to April, are highly recommended.

Perhaps best known of all the city's sporting events is the Emirates Airlines Dubai Sevens – three days of fine rugby in brilliant winter sun, washed down with beer (see p.228).

When you're not watching from the stands, there's plenty of opportunity to catch up on the games back home, as you'll find sports bars with big screen TVs everywhere (see Going Out, p.153). And don't be surprised by the sight of souk vendors milling around in Chelsea tops – this city can glory hunt with the best of them.

If sitting in a smoky bar isn't your idea of exercise then you can always head for the slopes. You can ski and snowboard every day in this sun-drenched town thanks to the wonder of Ski Dubai – the coolest fake slope in the world (see p.87).

If you prefer to get wet in more natural surroundings, there's some good waves off the coast of the UAE. While there's plenty of opportunity for low-key wakeboarding on the beaches of Dubai, serious surfers tend to prefer the swell and conditions in Oman (see p.102), especially Masirah Island.

For more on Dubai's annual sporting events see p.288.

Beach clubs

If your idea of sport is slapping on the factor 20 and lying in your speedos, then there are plenty of beaches in Dubai. Choose between one of the public beaches on Jumeria Road, or a beach park (see p.158). If you're not staying in a beachfront hotel and you fancy some watersports then your best bet is to get a day pass at one of the hotels. This will give you access to their sporting facilities and often includes lunch.

Watersports

Never mind the unsightly tight wetsuit, it's time to grab that board and start the engines. The Arabian Gulf awaits...

Diving in Dubai is definitely an experience you won't forget, but there are plenty of other ways to take to the water and have the time of your life. With such fabulous weather conditions, you should get your feet (and face) wet at least once during your stay.

Snorkelling is an amazingly serene way to explore the UAE's varied marine life and there are a few great spots. One of the most popular being the charming Snoopy Island, near the Sandy Beach Hotel in Dibba. Most tour operators (see p.95) will arrange day trips. Closer to Dubai, the sea off Jumeria Beach has a fair amount of coloured fish (you may even spot Nemo) should you just want a quick break from sunbathing. Most hotels and dive centres rent equipment (snorkel, mask and fins).

If you'd rather be above the waves there are plenty of opportunities to jetski, waterski, wakeboard and windsurf – all of which can be booked through your hotel or independent retailers on the public beaches. The average cost of jetskiing is Dhs.100 for half an hour. But before you climb aboard and start revving the engine, check that you're covered by your medical insurance.

Reefs and diving

Superb for all levels of diving, the UAE's coastal waters make for sweet respite from the often blistering sun.

Blessed with a rich underwater world, Dubai is a haven for diving enthusiasts. The year-round warm waters are home to an abundance of marine and coral life, with exotic, brightly coloured fish, mingling with rays, whale sharks, and turtles.

The UAE has two coasts to explore, so it's not likely you'll be hanging up your fins out of boredom. The shipwreck-rich west coast covers Abu Dhabi, Dubai and Sharjah, and to the east, where coral is king, lies Fujairah, Khor Fakkan and Dibba. Everything is easily accessible from Dubai – a road trip from coast to coast, taking in spectacular scenery, only takes a couple of hours.

The most popular sites on the west coast are *MV Sarraf 3*, Cement Barge, *MV Dara*, Port Rashid Wreck and Sheikh Mohammed's Barge. Depending on conditions, expect a visibility range of about five to 20 metres.

On the eastern side of the country, be sure to plunge and experience Martini Rock, a small underwater mountain covered with colourful soft coral. North of Khor Fakkan is the Car Cemetery. You may think placing 16 vehicles below water is a touch artificial, but this reef is thriving and one of the most popular in the region. If you're feeling particularly adventurous, take a trip to Mussandam, the northern most part of the UAE (though strictly a part of the neighbouring Sultanate of Oman and hence visiting the area requires a separate visa). Often described as the 'Norway of the Middle East', it's a stunning mix of fjords and sheer cliffs plunging directly into the sea.

There are lots of diving companies in Dubai and whether you are a dry-as-a-bone beginner or a seasoned diver looking to become an instructor, you won't have any problems finding a school that suits your needs. Courses are offered under the usual international training organisations such as PADI, CMAS, NAUI, IANTD and HAS. For more information on dive sites, grab a copy of the ***UAE Underwater Explorer***.

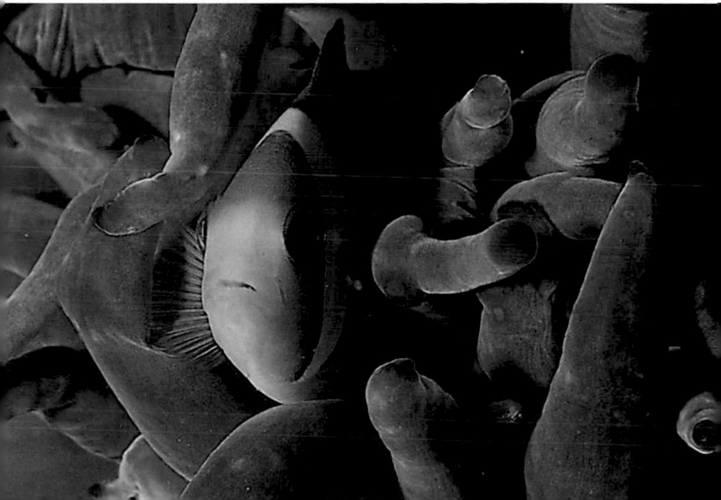

UAE dive centres

7 Seas Divers www.7seasdivers.com
P.O. Box 9878, Khor Fakkan
Phone: 09 238 7400 Fax: 09 238 7440

Al Boom Diving www.alboomdiving.com
Al Wasl Road, Dubai
Phone: 04 342 2994 Fax: 04 342 2995

Divers Down www.diverdown.net
Oceanic Hotel, Khor Fakkan
Phone: 09 237 0299 Fax: 09 237 0194

Emirates Diving Association www.emiratesdiving.com
Heritage & Diving Village, Shindaga, Dubai
Phone: 04 393 9390 Fax: 04 393 9391

Pavilion Dive Centre www.jumeirahinternational.com
The Jumeirah Beach Hotel, Dubai
Phone: 04 348 0000, 406 8827 Fax: 04 348 2273

Sandy Beach Diving Centre www.sandybm.com
Fujeirah
Phone: 09 244 5050/5354 Fax: 09 244 5900

Scuba 2000 www.scuba-2000.com
Al Badiya Beach, Fujeirah
Phone: 09 238 8477 Fax: 09 238 8478

Scuba Dubai www.scubadubai.com
Dubai
Phone: 04 331 7433 Fax: 04 331 0680

Scuba International www.scubainternational.net
Fujeirah
Phone: 09 220 0060 Fax: 09 222 0548

Scubatec www.scubatec.net
Karama, Dubai
Phone: 04 334 8988 Fax: 04 336 6461

Golf courses

Dubai's exotic desert provides the backdrop to some of the most spectacular and inspirational fairways in the world.

The paradox of majestic greens and superior facilities slap bang in the middle of the desert make 18 holes here a special attraction. And doesn't Dubai know it.

There's huge interest from the golfing world in the city's new and improving courses, helped greatly by the prestigious, Tiger Woods-attracting Dubai Desert Classic, being held in the city each March.

The three major hitters (Emirates Golf Club, where the Classic is played, Dubai Creek Golf Club and Nad Al Sheba Club) regularly host local tournaments and annual competitions which are open to all. New courses in the city include the exacting Desert Course at Arabian Ranches, designed with a little help from Jack Nicklaus.

It's worth noting a couple of things about golf in Dubai – namely that the higher-end 18-hole courses will insist that you bring along your handicap certificate before they allow you to play, and that almost every club is kitted out with at least a couple of coaches and the very latest technology to help improve your skills. A few places will hire out clubs and sometimes even shoes for the novices among you, but all at an extra fee.

Al Badia Golf Resort

04 285 5772

Al Rabat Street, Ras Al Khor www.albadiagolfresort.com

In the midst of the shopping frenzy that is Dubai Festival City lies this 7250-yard, par 72 course, designed around 11 lakes and waterfalls that lead into the nearby creek. The resort's high-tech swing analysis rooms cater for all levels, from beginner to scratch player.

Arabian Ranches Golf Club

04 366 3000

Arabian Ranches www.thedesertcourse.com

If you've got an official handicap then you should take on this beauty, designed by Ian Baker-Finch in partnership with Nicklaus design. The club is one of the few in Dubai to offer GPS

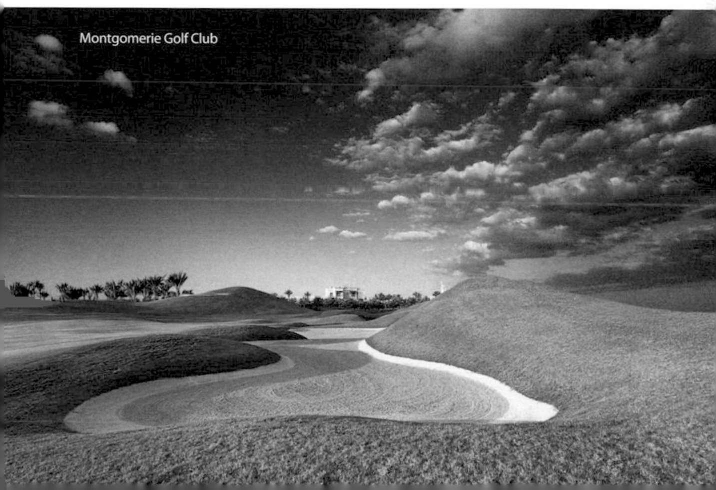

Montgomerie Golf Club

(global positioning system) on all its golf carts, allowing players to see the exact distance from their buggy to the centre of the green – sadly, it won't help you get the ball there.

Dubai Country Club

04 333 1155
Nr Bukadra interchange, Bukadra www.dubaicountryclub.com

The two sand courses on offer here make for a unique golfing experience, for both beginners and seasoned golfers more used to conventional grass fairways. The club holds the annual Dubai Men's Open, and it includes a 24-bay floodlit driving range and an area where you can practise putting on sand.

Emirates Golf Club

04 380 2222
Opp. Hard Rock Cafe www.dubaigolf.com

Originally known as the Desert Miracle when it first opened way back in 1988 as the region's first all-grass championship course, Emirates Golf Club is now well known for hosting the Dubai Desert Classics. With two 18-hole courses to choose from, you'll need to free up more than a morning for this gem.

Montgomerie Golf Club

04 390 5600
Emirates Hills www.themontgomerie.com

A slice of Scotland in the heart of the desert. Well, sort of. This course is set on 200 acres of land and was part designed by, you guessed it, Colin Montgomerie. Naturally, it includes the world's largest green (in the shape of the UAE, no less), alongside more traditional fairways.

Nad Al Sheba

04 336 3666

Nr Bu Kidra Interchange

www.nadalsheba.com

What do you mean you haven't played golf at night? This club offers the only known floodlit 18-hole course in the Middle East, with British PGA professionals on hand should you get lost in the dark. Oh, and if the fairways seem a tad familiar it's because they're based on the Old Course at the Home of Golf, St Andrews in Scotland.

Resort Course

04 883 6000

Jebel Ali Golf Resort & Spa

www.jebelali-international.com

With landscaped gardens and a spa only a stone's throw away, this retreat will compensate for the stress of your poor shot selection. A nine-hole, par-36 course for all levels of golfers, it comes with a cracking view of the Arabian Gulf. And don't be deterred by the short course; with four tees on each hole you can easily turn your game into an 18-hole round.

Dubai Creek Golf & Yacht Club

04 895 6000

Garhoud

www.dubaigolf.com

Playing here will require a handicap certificate, and with floodlit facilities, three practice greens and a 36-bay driving range, you can tell the course means business. If you're a newcomer to the game, you can join the Golf Academy, where PGA-qualified instructors are on hand for guidance in the golf studio with its state-of-the-art swing analysis software.

Spas and well-being

Where else would you go to unwind if not in one of the most indulgent cities in the world? Dubai is renowned for its luxury spa treatments, so you'll be looking after yourself in style.

You've bought enough old gold to start your own souk, you've seen the sights, day and night, and you're all out of little black dresses. It must be time to acquaint yourself with another side of Dubai life – the wind-down.

As you can tell from the sculpted bodies on the beach, beauty salons are incredibly popular in Dubai and you'll find spas cropping up all over the place. Most are found in the city's five-star hotels and there's a huge variety to choose from, each offering plenty of treatments. Services range from manicures, pedicures, waxing and henna, to the latest haircuts, styles and colours. And that's just for men. Yes, men's grooming is big, big business in Dubai, with new outlets opening all the time. Of course, salons offer fabulous services for both sexes, but best of all, prices are extremely competitive, whether you're having your chest waxed or your eyebrows tinted.

In true Dubai fashion, spa pampering is done with so much indulgence and decadence that you could spend whole weekends getting lost in a world of candles and comforting pan pipes. And once you've had that three-hour facial you'll be good for another round of lethal cocktails and late nights.

1847

Grosvenor House

04 399 8989

www.grosvenorhotel.com

In a city where the ladies seem to get all the best perks and pampering, it's about time the men fought back. Step forward 1847, the first dedicated 'grooming lounge' for men in the Middle East. Why not start with a manicure or pedicure (or both) in the privacy of your own 'study', where you can sit back and flick on your personal LCD TV, or swing open the adjoining doors and chat to your neighbour. Follow this with a traditional shave, and then end your day with a full-body massage in one of the welcoming candle-lit therapy suites.

Akaru Spa
04 282 8578

Aviation Club
www.aviationclubonline.com

The autumnal colours, glass features and wooden fittings make for a truly tranquil retreat at Akaru. Head for the dimly lit surroundings of the Turkish room for a sauna, and enjoy fresh fruit juices on tap. Try out one of the Thalgo (La Beaute Marine) options, which is a range of specialised 'body marine treatments' that sound like a posh dip in the sea. Or, in the cooler months, choose to take your facial and massage on the rooftop terrace.

Amara Spa
04 602 6100

Park Hyatt
www.dubai.park.hyatt com

No such thing as communal changing here, instead you are escorted directly to your treatment room which acts as your personal spa. You'll enjoy all the usual facilities, as well as a relaxation corner, and after your treatment, or during if you are having a scrub or wrap, you can treat yourself to your own private outdoor shower under the sun. A refreshing break from the same old spa routine.

Assawan Spa and Health Club
04 301 7777

Burj Al Arab
www.burj-al-arab.com

Located on the 18th floor of the breathtaking Burj Al Arab and aptly named after a stone that has magical soothing and invigorating properties, this place has an amazing list of treatments and therapies to smooth your cares away, including massage, facials and La Prairie treats. An appointment here will also give you license to the excellent hotel gym and studio.

Sports & Spas

Cleopatra's Spa

04 324 7700
Pyramid's, Wafi City
www.waficity.com

From the moment you don the big fluffy robe and wooden flip-flops at one of Dubai's oldest and largest days spas, you'll start to unwind. By the time you get to the herbal tea and warm bean bag at the end of your session, you'll be positively Zen-like. Never mind the naff gold statues, just feel the benefit of the signature milk bath.

Givenchy Spa/Oriental Hammam

04 399 9999
One&Only Royal Mirage
www.oneandonlyresort.com

You'll have a very difficult, if pleasant, decision to make at The One & Only Royal Mirage. Either you go for the private rooms at the Givenchy Spa, where a wide range of treatments and therapies include the Canyon Love Stone Therapy, an energy-balancing massage using warm and cool stones, and the highly recommended deep cleansing facials. Or it's the impressive Arabic architecture, and equally impressive time-honoured massages, steam baths and Jacuzzis at Oriental Hammam.

Health Club & Spa

04 343 8888
Shangri-La Hotel
www.shangri-la.com

Taking up the entire fourth floor of one of Dubai's most luxurious hotels, Health Club & Spa includes nine spa treatment rooms, a gym, outdoor swimming pools, Jacuzzi, plunge pools, movement studio, sauna and steam rooms. More than enough for any self-respecting spa junky.

Ritz-Carlton Spa

04 399 4000

Ritz-Carlton, Dubai — www.ritzcarlton.com

Although the Ritz-Carlton spa offers a contrasting range of Eastern, European and marine therapies, the Balinese massage is heaven personified – choose the level of pressure then catch that cloud. The facilities also include eight therapy rooms, Jacuzzi, sauna, steam room and a ladies' gym complete with toning tables. The Javanese Lulur full body treatment, which starts with a massage and ends with a body scrub and yoghurt moisturising, is the business.

Satori Spa

04 344 5333

Jumeriah Beach Club & Spa — www.jumeirahinternational.com

Sheltered by lush foliage, this spa is set in its own landscaped area, complete with outdoor Balinese shower, and offers an extensive range of therapies. The Satori Signature treatments are unique, and range from body wraps to reflexology and chakra balancing. Though exclusive to club members, guests are welcome and special day packages are available.

Six Senses Spa

04 366 6818

Madinat Jumeirah — www.jumeirahinternational.com

A quick abra ride from the bustling Madinat Souk takes you a world away to this tranquil, luxurious spa. With incredible attention to detail, Six Senses offers a range of holistic treatments that pamper, heal and energise. Stroll to your individual bungalow located amid landscaped grounds and prepare to relax and rejuvenate. There's also a fabulously healthy restaurant just a gentle stroll away.

Solesenses Spa

04 318 1904

Le Meridien Mina Seyahi

www.lemeridien.com

Housed in a small white building (blink and you'll miss it), separate from the hotel, this intimate spa has three treatment rooms and one make-up and manicure room, but no facilities such as a sauna or a steam room. The treatment range includes manicure, pedicure, waxing, self-tanning, reflexology and massages including Thai. All you have to do is lie back in comfy surroundings with low lighting and mellow music (you'll get to love Enya) and let the therapist work her magic. You'll come out 75 minutes later positively glowing, and feeling at least seven years younger.

Ladies' treatment room at Ritz-Carlton, Dubai.

Health Club & Spa at Shangri-La.

The Grand Spa

04 317 2134

Grand Hyatt Dubai www.dubai.grand.hyatt.com

What this spa lacks in size it makes up for in atmosphere and attention to detail. The changing room and adjacent relaxation area have dark wooden floors and walls and are lit by rows of candles, while the wet area is drizzled in rose petals and houses a Jacuzzi, plunge pool, sauna and steam room. The treatments cover the usual range, but it's the fusion packages that really hit the spot. You get to combine a massage, body or hand/feet treatment, facial and pilates or circuit training. Grand, indeed.

The Spa At Palm Tree Court

04 883 6000

Jebel Ali Golf Resort & Spa
www.jebelali-international.com

The swaying palm trees and unspoiled sandy beaches should help get you in the mood for serious relaxation. Nestled amid the serene gardens of the charming Jebel Ali resort, this spa offers a variety of treatments and holistic experiences to soothe the stress of a week's worth of mall abuse.

Willow Stream Spa

04 332 5555

The Fairmont Dubai www.fairmont.com

Decorated in Roman bath-style, this spa has a separate male and female facility, both complete with fully equipped and state-of-the-art treatment rooms that share a swimming pool and gym. It may not seem particularly big in size, but it's definitely quality over quantity. Full and half-day packages can be tailored to include a range of treatments.

Shopping

MERCATO

Spending money

Unfeasibly big shopping malls, atmospheric souks and sheer variety of choice make for a shopper's paradise.

If you're a card-bashing shopaholic you could easily spend your entire stay, and budget, in one of Dubai's gigantic malls. But if the mere sight of a shop assistant brings you out in a sweat, it's probably best to look away now.

Dubai's commitment to shopping is, frankly, frightening. Why relegate retail to mere therapy when you can dedicate whole months of the year to not one, but two mammoth shopping festivals?

From the city's ever-increasing number of space-age malls (the next always more spectacular than the last), to its ancient creek-side souks, there is a ridiculous variety of temptations on offer. Choose from designer labels, whole international department stores and down and dirty souvenir shops. And that's just in Deira.

Shopping is central to every new development in the city, meaning that malls will offer you every conceivable opportunity to part with your cash – whether it's on the fake slopes of Ski Dubai or in the serene surrounds of a world-renowned spa. Everything is open until at least 21:00, so time won't save your wallet, either. The huge popularity of Dubai's main malls (p.136) is evident by the bumper crowds of locals, especially on Friday evenings. Not all of them have come to shop; for some this is recreation, a lifestyle choice and family outing rolled into one. Such social gatherings are helped by the fact that most foodcourts in the malls don't just offer generic fastfood, but a good variety of decent cuisine.

Hotels also recognise the power of the mall and many provide shuttle buses direct to the door. Others simply decide to stick whole lanes of shops in their own lobbies.

The majority of the big US and European clothing brands can be found here, and the rest won't be too far behind. But that's not to say that there aren't pleasant surprises in store. There's a thriving independent retail scene, with the smaller malls, many of which line Beach Road in Jumeira, full of the weird and wonderful, as well as the exclusive and expensive.

Some (blessed) relief from the boundless bling comes in the shape of Dubai's famous souks. Smaller and less confusing than the majority found in the Middle East, they provide a stark contrast to indoor glitz, and should be right at the top of your shopping list. Whether it's gold, frankincense or matching carpets, the souks will have something for all budgets and tastes.

Souvenirs

Souvenirs in Dubai tend not to be locally made but are imported from the subcontinent, the rest of the Middle East, and Africa. Authentic pieces are rare and can be quite expensive but the vendor will usually tell you the origin of a piece if asked. The items available are representative of the mix of cultures and influences that have shaped the city.

It's advisable to dress more modestly when visiting the souks, which are usually open from 08:00 to 13:00 and 16:00 to 19:00, except on Fridays when they only open in the afternoon. If you have time and money left, get yourself to Sharjah, Dubai's neighbouring emirate, and visit Al Arsah Souk (p.151). If you're still looking for a splash of colour, spend some time in Dubai's local shopping districts where cash and cheap goods reign. Al Faheidi Street (p.146) is best known for electronic goods, Karama (p.146) for clothes and souvenirs, and Satwa (p.147) for fabrics and tailors. Like Dubai's souks, the shops in these areas close for a few hours in the afternoon.

While there are genuine bargains to be had, especially in the souks and during the two shopping festivals (Dubai Shopping Festival in January and February, and Summer Surprises held from June to September), the prices in many of Dubai's shops are comparable with those found elsewhere, despite being tax-free.

And one final bit of advice for would-be mallrats: don't come dressed for the beach as the air con can be seriously cold, especially in summer.

Refunds and exchanges

The policy on refunds and exchanges varies from shop to shop. Refunds, even for faulty items, are uncommon in Dubai. It is more likely that an exchange will be offered, and a receipt, and often the original packaging, will be required. Also don't presume that you can exchange an item from an international brand when you get home. Always ask the store manager to clarify their policy.

Shopping

Dubai's best buys

Gold

With jewellery shops in every mall, every shopping street, and also in many hotels, it's little wonder that Dubai struggles to shake off its tag as 'the City of Gold'. The bright stuff is sold according to the daily gold rate, with an additional charge for craftsmanship, so there's limited flexibility on price. Always ask for a discount, but be prepared for it to be no higher than 5%. A popular choice of gift is to have a name translated into Arabic and then made up in gold. To avoid Steve becoming Sheila when you return home, ask an Arabic speaker to translate for you in advance.

Carpets

Styles of carpet vary depending on the country of origin, be it Iran, Pakistan, China or Central Asia, but so does quality, so it's advisable to do some research before you settle on an expensive shagpile. The carpet's origin, intricacy of the design, its material and whether it is machine made or handwoven will all dictate its value. But there are pieces to suit all pockets, from woven coasters to large silk carpets – just decide on the style and what you are willing to spend, and get haggling.

Pashminas

With shelves struggling under the weight of pashminas in many shops, it's almost impossible to pick one in less than three hours. Luckily, staff are prepared to take their premises apart until you find the perfect shade, so don't feel too much pressure. Most pashminas are a cotton/silk mix and their ratio dictates the price. It's a good idea to compare a few shops before buying as prices vary, and, as with most items, the more you buy the cheaper they become.

Shisha pipes

You'll find the iconic shisha pipe on sale everywhere, from Carrefour supermarkets to the streets of Karama and Satwa. The fruity tobacco, which comes in a variety of flavours, is also widely available. A good option for your more laidback friends.

Furniture

Wooden furniture is good value in Dubai and while you may not want to ship home a coffee table made out of an Arabian door, there are some great smaller items to be found, especially in Al Quoz, the industrial area between interchanges three and four on Sheikh Zayed Road.

Al Quoz is home to a number of furniture warehouses, many of which sell pieces crafted from Indonesian teak.

One of the best and most reasonable is Marina Gulf Trading (04 340 1112). For other independent stores, see p.146.

Keep the khanjar

If you buy a traditional dagger, the khanjar, it will need to be packed in your luggage to go in the hold – even if it's been framed – and you may still need to declare it. If it is in your hand luggage it will be confiscated. Check with your airline before you fly regarding their policy.

Main malls

Seen one shopping mall, seen them all? Not in Dubai. Here, you can snowboard, take a sauna or slump in front of an IMAX screen even before you browse the shops.

Deira City Centre

Map 1-F4
Garhoud
04 295 1010

Whereas newer malls try to carve out a niche amid Dubai's crowded shopping scene, City Centre sticks to its tried and trusted eclecticism. From a postcard to a Persian carpet, and Massimo Dutti to Mexx, you can buy anything here. And with the jewellery and textiles courts, as well as Arabian Treasures, for local furniture and homeware, you won't leave without a souvenir or seven. Designer-label devotees should head to Bin Hendi Avenue and its range of boutiques, couch potatoes for the electronics on the ground floor. Kids even have their very own Magic Planet. Hugely popular, especially at weekends, City Centre is well known by all taxi drivers, and many hotels provide a shuttle bus straight to its doors. There is even a left luggage area on the second floor.

BurJuman Centre

Map 1-E2
Bur Dubai
04 352 0222

Renowned in the city for its blend of high-street names and designer brands, BurJuman is where you head for a new wardrobe. Redeveloped in recent years, it's a slick and stylish mall – thanks largely to its branch of Saks Fifth Avenue, the legendary New York department store. But even if the price tags at Prada, Ralph Lauren and Paul Smith put you off, you'll find mid-price favourites in Zara, Mango and Next. There are plenty of jewellery, homeware and entertainment options, too. The cafes are good for coffee and a crafty peek at the passing fashionistas, and with play areas for kids (on the 3rd floor), plentiful taxis and parking, stress won't stop you shopping. BurJuman is only a short taxi ride from the creek, should you be sightseeing earlier or later in the day.

BurJuman Centre

Souk Madinat Jumeirah

Map 2-D1
Umm Suqeim 04 366 8888

This recreation of a traditional Middle Eastern marketplace is no cheesy theme mall. One wrong move in its narrow alleyways and it's every inch a real souk. Amid the bustle of its congested (and at times confusing) lanes, you'll find Dubai's biggest selection of speciality outlets selling the city's widest range of art and photography, among them the outstanding Gallery One. Elsewhere the emphasis is on more unusual brands (Tommy Bahamas and Celine Fashion, anyone?). Once you're done with wandering, let Madinat's impressive range of waterfront bars and restaurants take the strain.

Souk Madinat Jumeirah

Ibn Battuta

Off map

The Gardens, New Dubai

04 362 1900

So big that you'll need a guided tour to navigate its six courts, Ibn Battuta is part shopping mall, part history lesson, and 100% bonkers. Each court is themed on a country or region which at one time was visited by Ibn Battuta, a 14th century explorer. So you can nip into Egypt Court for a new pair of Adidas trainers, head over to India Court for that Daniel Hechter shirt, then settle down for three courses in China Court. A little further north, Andalusia is where you'll find life's essentials, while Tunisia will keep the kids occupied. Miss something in Egypt and it could be a long haul back. But unlike Battuta you've got the luxury of a taxi to ferry you back and forth.

Wafi Mall

Map 1-D5

Umm Hurair

04 324 4555

With its airy layout and sparsely filled walkways, the Pyramid-themed Wafi has more than a whiff of exclusivity. No wonder Raffles Hotel will be opening here soon. With a wide range of jewellery and couture, including Versace, Nicole Farhi, Tag Heuer, Gant, and Tiffany and Co, it boasts one of the city's biggest selections of designer names. For those looking for more down-to-earth goods, the large branch of Marks & Spencer shouldn't disappoint. Despite its mainly adult-sized prices, Wafi is also great for kids, with any number of fantastically named zones, including the hugely popular Encounter Zone. The Mall is part of the bigger Wafi City complex, so if you feel the need for pampering – or a pig out – simply head across to the Pyramid's Restaurants and Spa.

Mall of the Emirates

Map 2-D2

Al Barsha

04 341 4747

Stretching the concept of a shopping centre til it snaps, Mall of the Emirates lives up to its slightly pompous name. Inside the largest mall outside North America you'll find the Middle East's first dry ski slope, a five-star Kempinski hotel and a community theatre and arts centre. The 400-odd shops aren't bad either. There's plenty of designer labels (Burberry, Dolce & Gabbana, Versace), a great range of homewear (Marina Gulf, The ONE, Zara Home) and Harvey Nichols, London's achingly cool department store. Best of all, this behemoth is actually easy to navigate.

Mall of the Emirates

Mercato

Jumeira — Off map — 04 344 4161

Standing proud on Jumeira Beach Road, Mercato and its Renaissance-style architecture is hard to miss. With over 90 shops, restaurants and cafes, it is by far the biggest mall in fashionable Jumeira. It's all held together by the big boys of Spinneys (supermarket), Home Centre (home decor) and a large Virgin Megastore. Fashion stores range from the reasonably priced Pull and Bear and Top Shop, to Hugo Boss and Armani. Other favourites include Susan Walpole, which sells a range of locally inspired silk paintings, and Pride of Kashmir, which is good for local furniture and fabrics. There's also the brilliant Barbie Avenue, a whole shop dedicated to the queen of plastic dolls. When you're peckish, be sure to visit PAUL, the excellent patisserie, or the ever-reliable Fiesta Café.

Festival City

Garhoud — Off map

The newest kid on the already-crowded block is big even by Dubai's chunky standards. Currently under construction beside the creek in Deira, Festival City will be a beast of a retail, residential and leisure complex, boasting 450 shops and 90 restaurants. It will include Kid's World, the Waterfront Souk and a retail park that already houses the largest IKEA store in the Middle East. Among the names to have joined the Swedish giant are ACE Hardware, and the brilliantly named HyperPanda supermarket. Fans of four wheels can look forward to some of the world's largest car showrooms, from Toyota among others.

Other malls

Al Ghurair City

Map 1-F3

Deira

04 222 5222

Given a well-needed lick of paint a few years back, Dubai's oldest mall now houses an eight-screen cinema and international names like BHS and French Connection. But there's still a traditional atmosphere amid its maze-like two storeys, where you'll find abayas and dishdashas on sale.

Boulevard at Emirates Towers

Map 1-B3

Trade Centre 2

04 319 8999

Boulevard's designers stores include Cartier, Gucci, Jimmy Choo, and Villa Moda, which is so exclusive that it has its own entrance from the car park. If you're looking to unwind, there's also a health club and a branch of 1847, Dubai's first men-only spa.

Jumeirah Centre

Map 1-B1

Jumeria

04 379 9702

This is a good spot for souvenir shopping after a hard day's lounging on the beach. Chintzy names aside, Panache and Sunny Days offer good craft and gift items, whie the stationery shop on the ground floor has a decent range of art supplies should your creative juices be flowing.

Jumeirah Plaza

Map 1-B1

Jumeira

04 379 7111

That'll be the pink mall on Beach Road, outstanding for more than just its garish colour. Notable shops include House of Prose, an excellent second-hand bookshop and Heat Waves, where you can buy UV protection beachwear.

Lamcy Plaza

Map 1-D4

Oud Metha

04 335 9999

The tacky waterfall and rope-climbing clown inside the main entrance sum up Lamcy's haphazard charm. The only mall in Dubai to open seven days a week, it's five floors of open-plan shopping, packed full of bargains, practicality and the wonderfully named kids play area, Loulou Al Dugong's.

Palm Strip

Map 1-B1

Jumeira

04 376 1462

Where else but in Jumeira would you find a walk-in nail bar? N-Bar is just one of a number of independent boutiques making up the Strip. Wedged between Jumeirah Mosque and the public beach, it's a post-beach arcade with a number of speciality shops selling Arabic perfume and chocolate.

Reef Mall

Off Map

Deira

04 224 2240

Popular hangout for locals on the Deira side of the creek, Reef Mall is home to several big stores, including Home Centre, Lifestyle, Splash and The Baby Shop. There's also a huge Fun City, where kids can burn off their enthusiasm.

Town Centre Jumeirah

Off Map

Jumeira

04 374 0111

The pick of Town Centre's cafes is Café Ceramique, where you can paint a piece of pottery while you pick at your lunch (the piece will be fired on site and should be ready within a week). There's also a very useful little Empost (post office) counter here.

Outside the malls

Cheap, cheerful and full of character, Dubai's more traditional shopping areas are a bargain hunter's paradise.

Al Faheidi Street — Map 1-E2

Bur Dubai

Miles and miles of neon lighting betray the shopping focus of this bustling street. Al Faheidi should really be known as the 'electronics souk', packed as it is with global brands selling everything from laptops to the latest flat-screen TVs.

Prices here are competitive, but the vendors know the value of what they're selling. Still, it's a good place to put those well-honed bargaining skills to the test. It's also worth checking out some of the electronics chains in the malls, where you'll get a warranty and better customer service if something is wrong with your item.

Karama — Map 1-E3

Bur Dubai

A million miles from Mall of the Emirates, Karama is one of the city's oldest residential districts and easily the best place to find a bargain, especially if you need a new tracksuit or mosque alarm clock. It shouldn't take you long to realise the reason for the area's popularity and notoriety, as you are offered 'designer' watches and handbags at every turn. If you show even a hint of interest, you'll be whisked into a back room to view the booty. The invitations from every shop that you pass can get tiresome but

a simple 'no thank you,' normally does the trick. The main shopping area is the Al Karama Complex, a long street running through the middle of the district. It is lined by veranda-covered shops on both sides, with a range of t-shirts, shoes, shorts, and sunglasses, available at very reasonable prices. Be aware that much of the clothing comes from the Far East, so check the sizes before you buy the skinny fit. Should you have lost your flip-flops in the sea, you can pick up dirt cheap replacements, as well as other bargains, at Sana Fashion.

Satwa

Map 1-B2

Bur Dubai

Easily accessible by bus or taxi, Satwa is one of Dubai's original shopping areas, and something of a hidden treasure. Satwa's shops tend towards the lower end of the market but that's half the charm of this, the most bohemian quarter of Dubai. It's renowned for its reliable tailors and fabric shops, the pick of which is Deepaks, where the range is staggering and the prices extremely reasonable.

Independent shops

Various locations

As well as the main shopping districts and identikit malls, there is a growing independent shopping scene in Dubai. Whether you're looking for organic tomatoes, a linen suit or the latest release from your favourite German DJ, you won't be disappointed.

Fabindia (04 398 9633) on Al Mankhool Road, is great for cotton clothes, soft furnishings and materials direct from

India, all at very reasonable prices. Five Green in Oud Metha (04 336 4100) is arguably the best independent clothes shop in Dubai. As well as staging a number of 'street' art exhibtions, it sells creations from Dubai-based designers as well as labels including Paul Frank, GSUS and Boxfresh. If you'd rather something a little less baggy, there are a number of fine and very cheap tailors in Dubai. Among the most reliable are Dream Girl (04 337 7287 Karama, 04 349 5445 Satwa), good for anything from trousers to ball gowns, and Kachins (04 352 1386), recommended for their shirts and suits.

If you're looking to spruce up your home, there are number of good options, including Marina Gulf Trading (04 340 1112), a warehouse stuffed full of Indian and Indonesian furniture, with the odd silk thrown in, and Art of Life, which sells a range of oriental-inspired items and is a pleasant antidote to the formulaic furniture shops elsewhere in the city. At the top of the range, is The ONE with its more contemporary offerings and whose branches can be found in various malls. Its store in Jumeira also has a fantastic cafe selling freshly squeezed juices and great cakes. On a similarly healthy tip, there's the Organic Food & Cafe (04 398 9410) on Mankhool Road in Satwa and in The Greens. The food comes direct from the farmer and is free of any nasty interference – perfect if you need to cleanse after a week of high-carb grazing. It's unlikely that you'll spend your time in Dubai appreciating its independent music scene, but if you're overcome with an urge for vinyl then head to Ohm Records (04 397 3728) in Bur Dubai. Comfy sofas, practise decks and super-friendly staff make it a joy.

Souks and markets

If you're looking for the heartbeat of Dubai retail, head towards the creek and be prepared to haggle.

Fish Market

Map 1-F1

Deira

If you want to know what the fish you had for dinner really looks like, head to the fabulous Fish Market in Deira. The range of seafood on display is hugely impressive, but it's the theatre of the working market that will linger in your memory, and nostrils, long after the sight of red snapper.

Watch the traders haggle over their catch, then study the intricate cleaning and gutting process (just make sure you leave the open-toed sandals at home) to get a rare glimpse of one of Dubai's traditional crafts.

The best time to visit is early in the morning or late at night when the catch is coming in. Alongside the market there's a good seafood restaurant and a fantastic museum charting Dubai's fishing heritage.

Gold Souk

Map 1-F1

Deira

Whether you're looking for a one-off purchase to wow your loved-one, or just want to stare at expensive sparkly things, a visit to Dubai's best-known souk is essential. Wander through its meandering streets, lined with shops selling gold, silver, pearls

and precious stones, and wonder how far those dirhams will stretch. If it's gold you're after, don't expect a massive discount. It is sold by weight and according to the daily international price, so prices will be much the same as in the shops and malls. Of course this is not taking into account your (excellent) bargaining skills. Be aware that most of the outlets here operate split shifts, so try not to visit between 13:00 and 16:00.

Spice Souk

Map 1-F2

Deira

With its narrow side streets and wonderful aromas, the Spice Souk is a pleasant taste of pre-skyscraper Dubai. Sure, the number of spice shops may have diminished in recent years, but the atmosphere remains as intoxicating. Most of the stalls sell a very similar range, but the vendors are usually happy to offer advice on the types of spices and their uses. And you could bag some saffron at a bargain price. Most stores operate split shifts so mornings and evenings are the best time to visit.

Textile Souk

Map 1-E1

Bur Dubai

This ever-popular souk in Bur Dubai imports textiles from all over the world, with many of the more elaborate items coming from the subcontinent and the Far East. There are silks and satins in an amazing array of colours and patterns, velvets and intricately embroidered fabrics. Meena Bazaar is the shop that most taxi drivers head for, and they have an amazing selection. Be prepared to haggle – prices are always negotiable and there are often sales, particularly around the major holidays, Eid and Divali, and the shopping festivals. Basic cottons are harder to find but you can always try Satwa (p.30).

Al Arsah Souk (Sharjah)

Formerly the heart of Sharjah city, Al Arsha Souk is the most traditional souk in the emirate. Around 100 tiny shops line a labyrinth of peaceful alleyways, selling goods including silver jewellery, perfumes, spices, coffee pots and wedding chests. When you need a break, there's an Arabic coffee shop by the central courtyard. The souk is open from 09:00 to 13:00 and 16:30 to 20:30/22:00, and closed Friday mornings. Be aware that timings vary from shop to shop.

Central Souk (Sharjah)

One glimpse of the beautifully designed azure tiles here and you'll see why this is called 'Blue Souk'. Its ground floors have a mix of shops, not unlike those found in Karama (p.146), selling jewellery, clothing, electronics and textiles. The upper floors are where you'll find Omani and Yemeni antique jewellery. There is something to suit all budgets, from camel saddle bags, to incredibly intricate silk carpets worth tens of thousands of dirhams.

Shopping in Sharjah

Be aware that Sharjah is more conservative than Dubai, so it is courteous to dress more modestly. It should take around 30 to 45 minutes to reach the Sharjah souks from Bur Dubai but the traffic can be pretty heavy, so try to travel outside rush hours. If you prefer to shop without the crowds, visit in the mornings.

Going Out

Planet food

Few cities can compete with Dubai when it comes to cosmopolitan cuisine. Whether it's Vietnamese, Arabic, Indian or Italian, this city has room for all budgets and belt sizes.

If you struggle with indecision each time the waiter comes to the table, then get ready for more awkward shuffling. Dubai offers its visitors such a staggering choice of cuisines in so many spectacular settings that it's often hard to know where to look.

But that's not to say that it's five-star fine dining all the way; some of the best food in the city is still found on the streets of 'old' Dubai in authentic Arabic and Indian restaurants. And in this chapter you'll find independent reviews of places to suit both budgets. You'll also find information and insight on a range of cafes, bars, pubs and clubs, as Dubai continues its quest to own the Middle East party crown.

Many of Dubai's most popular restaurants are located within hotels and leisure clubs and these are virtually the only outlets where you can drink alcohol with your meal. But the city's independent restaurants should never be ignored just because they're dry.

When eating out be aware you may end being charged a service charge *and* municipality tax, so always check the bottom of your bill. And if you tip the waiter directly, try and ensure it goes to them and not straight in the cash register.

the
noodle house

Bur Dubai & Karama

Street life here is a mix of local dwellers dining for less than 10 dirhams, shisha aficionados and punters on the prowl for discount booze.

Barry's Bench

Mexican

Arabian Courtyard Hotel

04 351 6646

It's well worth making the trip to Bur Dubai for this new Tex-Mex. Although independent, Barry's Bench is licensed thanks to its location within the Arabian Courtyard Hotel, which means you can wash down the hearty food with margharitas. Map A 1

Basta Art Cafe

Cafe

Bastakiya

04 353 5071

Long-term resident of Bastakiya, this quaint, bohemian cafe has recently opened a sister branch in Arabian Ranches. Both are similar in style, with wicker tables and chairs on a laidback terrace, and offer splendid juices and smart salads. Map A 2

Bastakiya Nights

Arabic

Nr Rulers Court

04 353 7772

This restaurant is a well thought-out celebration of Arabia. Not only is the food excellent, but the surroundings couldn't be more stylishly authentic – there's a choice of private rooms, a beautiful central courtyard and, best of all, a rooftop offering stunning views across the blur of Bur Dubai. Map A 3

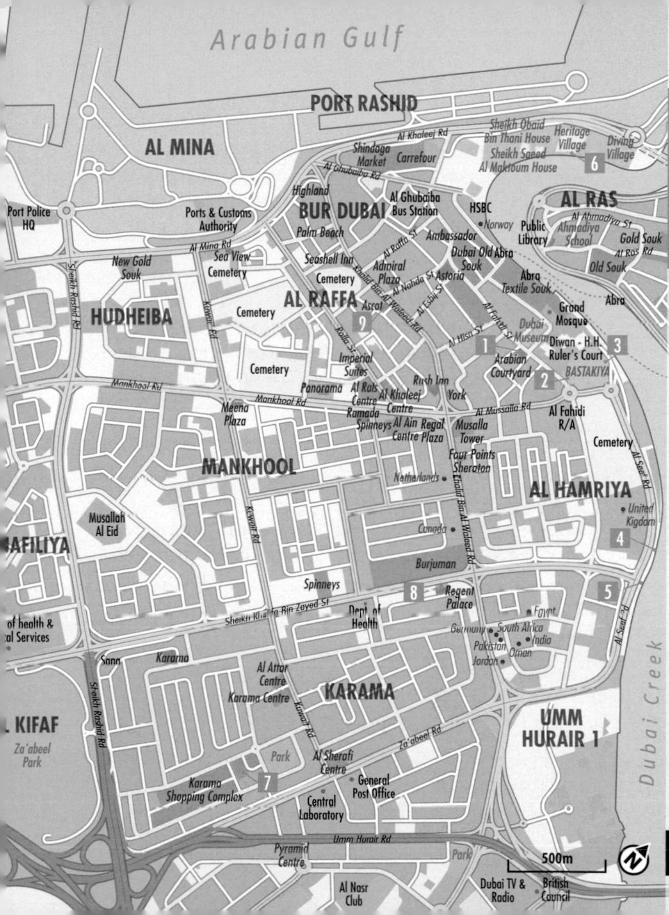

Arabian Gulf

PORT RASHID

AL MINA

Al Khaleej Rd

Sheikh Obaid Bin Thani House

Heritage Village

Diving Village

Shindaga Market

Carrefour

Sheikh Saeed Al Maktoum House

6

Al Ghubaiba Rd

Highland

Al Ghubaiba Bus Station

AL RAS

Port Police HQ

Ports & Customs Authority

BUR DUBAI

HSBC

Norway

Public Library

Al Ahmadiya St

Ahmadiya School

Gold Souk

Palm Beach

Ambassador

Al Ras Rd

Al Mina Rd

Sea View

Seashell Inn

Al Raffa St

Dubai Old Souk

Abra

Old Souk

New Gold Souk

Cemetery

Admiral Plaza

Astoria

Abra

Textile Souk

Cemetery

Khalid Bin Al Waleed Rd

Al Nahda St

Al Esbij St

Abra

HUDHEIBA

Cemetery

AL RAFFA

Ascot

Grand Mosque

Sheikh Rashid Rd

Kuwait Rd

9

Al Fahidi St

Dubai Museum

Raffa St

Al Hisn St

1

Diwan - H.H. Ruler's Court

3

Imperial Suites

Arabian Courtyard

Cemetery

BASTAKIYA

Mankhool Rd

Panorama

Al Rais Centre

Rush Inn

2

Al Khaleej Centre

York

Mankhool Rd

Meena Plaza

Ramada

Al Mussalla Rd

Al Fahidi R/A

Spinneys

Al Ain Regal Centre Plaza

Musalla Tower

Cemetery

Four Points Sheraton

MANKHOOL

Al Seef Rd

Netherlands

AL HAMRIYA

United Kingdom

Musallah Al Eid

Canada

4

Kuwait Rd

Khalid Bin Al Waleed Rd

AFILIYA

Burjuman

Spinneys

8

Regent Palace

5

Sheikh Khalifa Bin Zayed St

Dept of Health

Egypt

of health & cal Services

Germany

South Africa

India

Al Seef Rd

Pakistan

Oman

Sana

Karama

Jordan

Al Attar Centre

Karama Centre

KARAMA

Dubai Creek

Kuwait Rd

UMM HURAIR 1

KIFAF

Sheikh Rashid Rd

Za'abeel Park

Za'abeel Rd

Park

Al Sherafi Centre

General Post Office

Karama Shopping Complex

7

Central Laboratory

Umm Hurair Rd

Pyramid Centre

Park

500m

N

A

Al Nasr Club

Dubai TV & Radio

British Council

Bateaux Dubai

Dinner Cruise

Nr British Embassy

04 399 4994

Bateuaux's mainly French menu, which is overseen by an ex-Orient Express chef, is small but surprisingly good considering the usual cruise fare. And the glass-topped boat makes for a classy way to cruise through the creek. Map A 4

Danat Dubai Cruises

Dinner Cruise

Bastakiya

04 351 1117

All dishes here are cooked around a live cooking station, but that's not the only entertainment – there's also a dinky dance floor should you feel the need to cut loose. But it's really the view of the creek at night that makes this worth the effort. Map A 5

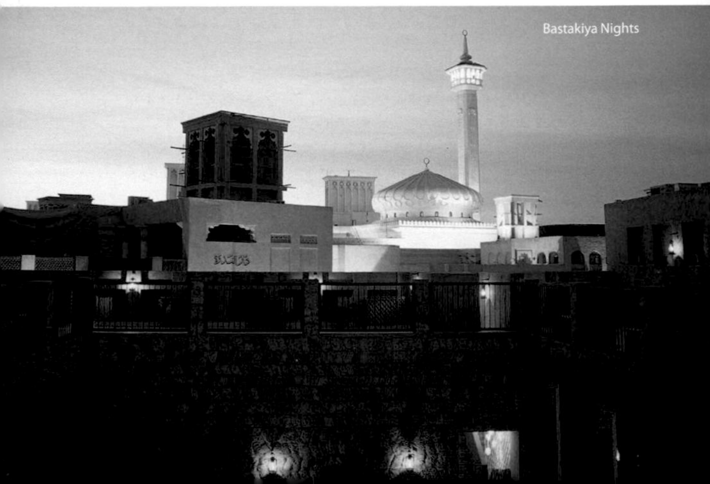

Bastakiya Nights

Kan Zaman

Arabic/Lebanese

Heritage & Diving Village

04 393 9913

Kan Zaman offers some of the best night views of the creek, an excellent Arabic menu, and big-sized portions with small-size price tags. Iranian, Chinese and Western dishes are also available at similarly reasonable prices. Map A 6

Karachi Darbar

Pakistani

Karama

04 267 3131

Quite possibly the cheapest place in Dubai for tasty, good quality food, this Indo-Pakistani chain is a big favourite with locals. The no-nonsense but friendly service, the range of food and the generous portions make this one of Karama's finest. Map A 7

Rock Bottom Café

Bar/Nightclub

Regent Palace Hotel

04 396 3888

This staple of Bur Dubai nightlife undergoes a transformation as the evening progresses. Early on it passes for a quiet restaurant, with couples and families enjoying reasonably priced meals at candle-lit tables. By night, it turns into a monster as the live band and local DJ draw an uncordinated crowd of mad-for-it binge drinkers. Map A 8

Waxy O'Conner's

Bar

Ascot Hotel

04 352 0900

This faux Irish favourite has all the usual suspects (big screen TVs, a pool table, predictable bangers and mash, fish and chips, and burgers). It regularly offers lots of specials, including a 'Freaky Friday Brunch' with hangover-inducing prices. Map A 9

Deira & the creek

Whether it's fine dining with great views of the creek or a dance in a sweaty club where the drinks come in pairs, Dubai's oldest neighbourhood doesn't disappoint.

Al Dawaar
International

Hyatt Regency Hotel
04 317 2222

Panoramic views of Dubai are not the only reasons for visiting Al Dawaar, the city's only revolving restaurant – its international buffet and assortment of desserts rate highly, too. Discreet service lets you concentrate on the ever-changing scenery. Map B 1

Ashiana
Indian

Sheraton Dubai Creek Hotel
04 207 1733

Serving steaming, delectable platefuls of authentic dishes from all regions of India, Ashiana has a well-deserved reputation as one of the finest Indian restaurants in Dubai. The decor and service both reflect the best of a vibrant subcontinent. Map B 2

Bamboo Lagoon
Far Eastern

JW Marriott Hotel
04 262 4444

With a good range of Asian-Pacific cuisine and its tropical garden theme, Bamboo Lagoon is a slice of island life in the middle of the desert. Live cooking stations are dotted around the paths and ponds, tempting you to reach out for a quick nibble. Just mind the grass-skirted singers seranading the next table. Map B 3

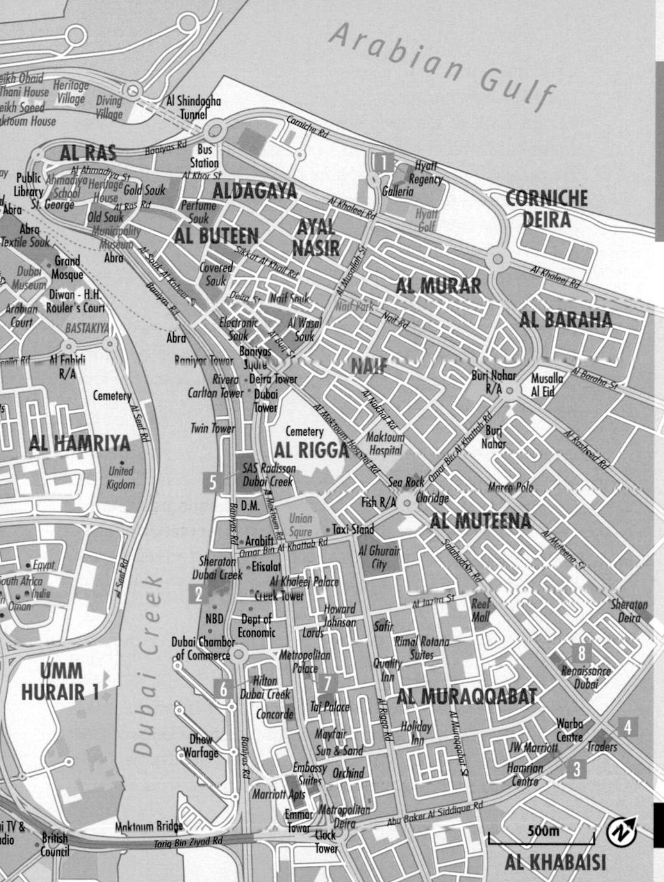
Arabian Gulf
Sheikh Obaid bin Thani House
Heritage Village
Diving Village
Sheikh Saeed Maktoum House
Al Shindagha Tunnel
Corniche Rd
AL RAS
Baniyas Rd
Bus Station
1
Hyatt Regency
Galleria
Al Ahmadiya St
Al Khor St
Public Library
Ahmadiya School
Heritage House
Gold Souk
St. George
Al Ras Rd
ALDAGAYA
Al Khaleej Rd
CORNICHE DEIRA
Hyatt Golf
Old Abra
Perfume Souk
Old Souk
Abra
Textile Souk
Municipality Museum
AL BUTEEN
AYAL NASIR
Sikkat Al Khail Rd
Al Musallah St
Abra
Dubai Museum
Grand Mosque
Al Souk Al Kabeer St
Covered Souk
Al Khaleej Rd
AL MURAR
Diwan - H.H. Ruler's Court
Arabian Court
Baniyas Rd
Deira St
Naif Souk
Naif Park
Naif Rd
AL BARAHA
BASTAKIYA
Electronic Souk
Al Wasal Souk
Abra
Al Buri St
Al Fahidi R/A
Baniyas Tower
Baniyas Squre
NAIF
Burj Nahar R/A
Musalla Al Eid
Al Baraha St
Rivera
Deira Tower
Cemetery
Carlton Tower
Dubai Tower
Al Nakhal Rd
Al Seef Rd
Al Maktoum Hospital Rd
Omar Bin Al Khattab Rd
Burj Nahar
Al Rashidiya Rd
Twin Tower
Cemetery
Maktoum Hospital
AL HAMRIYA
AL RIGGA
United Kingdom
SAS Radisson Dubai Creek
5
Sea Rock
Marco Polo
Al Maktoum Rd
Fish R/A
Claridge
D.M.
AL MUTEENA
Union Squre
Taxi Stand
Baniyas Rd
Arabift
Omar Bin Al Khattab Rd
Al Ghurair City
Al Muteena St
Salahuddin Rd
Egypt
Sheraton Dubai Creek
Etisalat
South Africa
India
Oman
Al Seef Rd
2
Al Khaleej Palace
Creek Tower
Al Jazira St
Reef Mall
Sheraton Deira
Dubai Creek
NBD
Dept of Economic
Howard Johnson
Lords
Safir
Rimal Rotana Suites
Dubai Chamber of Commerce
Metropolitan Palace
8
UMM HURAIR 1
Quality Inn
Renaissance Dubai
6
Hilton Dubai Creek
7
Concorde
Taj Palace
AL MURAQQABAT
Al Rigga Rd
Al Muraqqabat St
Dhow Wharfage
Baniyas Rd
Mayfair
Holiday Inn
Warba Centre
4
Sun & Sand
JW Marriott
Traders
Embassy Suites
Orchind
Hamrian Centre
3
Marriott Apts
Emmar Tower
Metropolitan Deira
Abu Baker Al Siddique Rd
Dubai TV & Radio
British Council
Maktoum Bridge
Tariq Bin Ziyad Rd
Clock Tower
500m
AL KHABAISI

Chameleon
Bar

Traders Hotel Dubai
04 265 9888

Vibrant cocktail bar with changing drinks menu and regular entertainment (get it?). Booze is reasonably cheap and there are the obligatory two free drinks for ladies. The cocktail menu has enough variety to have you licking your lips, rolling your eyes, and climbing the walls. Map B 4

The China Club
Chinese

SAS Radisson Dubai Creek
04 205 7333

With 11 master chefs preparing some Chinese dishes that even the most die-hard fan of the cuisine hasn't heard of, you might be puzzled by the menu, but not the quality of the food. A great place for group dining, with excellent service. Map B 5

Creekside
Japanese

Sheraton Dubai Creek Hotel
04 207 1750

This welcoming Japanese eatery keeps its patrons coming back again and again, thanks to quality food served in chilled surroundings. The sushi is sublime, while the teppanyaki live-cooking stations raise a smile. A variety of theme nights throughout the week offer decent value. Map B 2

Cucina
Italian

JW Marriott
04 262 4444

Thanks to its rustic, Tuscan decor and traditional menu, Cucina is consistently popular and a pleasant change from Dubai's usual glitz. Excellent pizzas and pastas can be washed down with a good bottle from the reasonably priced wine list. Map B 3

Clockwise from top: Al Dawaar, Cucina, Glasshouse.

The Fish Market

Seafood

SAS Radisson Dubai Creek

04 205 7333

This may be a fish restaurant, but there's a catch – you, accompanied by a member of staff clad in plastic gloves and clutching a wicker shopping basket, select your fresh fish and other ingredients courtesy of mother nature. Then sit back and let the chef do the hard bit. Map B 5

Glasshouse – Brasserie

European

Hilton Dubai Creek

04 227 1111

Get a taste of the Mediterranean at this chic brasserie, where large windows offer pleasant views of the creek. There's a decent wine list and extensive vegetarian options, but just watch the glass floor – it'll make you wobbly after too much sangria. Map B 6

Hofbrauhaus

German

JW Marriott

04 262 4444

Overflowing steins of hand-crafted beer and man-sized portions of succulent, meaty fare are the staples of Hofbrauhaus. A warm atmosphere, helped by the booze, and piped oompah music add to the feeling that you're in Munchen. As does the German waiter in Lederhosen. Map B 3

JW's Steakhouse

Steakhouse

JW Marriott

04 262 4444

Chefs can be seen cleaving huge chunks of meat in the open kitchen, and sure enough, the US Angus cuts are the real thing (stick to the fillet if you are fussy about tenderness). The menu also has a few good seafood options. Map B 3

La Moda

Italian

SAS Radisson Dubai Creek 04 205 7333

Large groups in a party mood will love La Moda, with its chilled vibe and delicious choice of pizzas and pastas, not to mention staff dressed in bizarre, orange 'pit crew' overalls. It's just a pity that the food is slightly overpriced. Map B 5

Miyako

Japanese

Hyatt Regency Hotel 04 317 2222

One of Dubai's top Japanese restaurants, Mikyako is filled with repeat customers. It's certainly not Dubai's cheapest option, but the flavours are subtle, and the standards the same as you'd expect from a superior Tokyo restaurant. Worth the extra dirhams. Map B 1

Palm Grill

Steakhouse

SAS Radisson Dubai Creek 04 257 3333

Serving succulent steaks from Australia, Palm Grill prepares its dishes to your specific demands, and the chefs seem to get it right every time. Although it's expensive, it's easily one of the finest grills in town. Map B 5

Shabestan

Persian

SAS Radisson Dubai Creek 04 257 3333

Elegant hospitality and sumptuous, traditional cuisine are the main selling points of this excellent venue. While the range of authentic dips, soups, kebabs and stews should enchant even the most well-travelled palate. Map B 5

Shabestan

Sketch

International

Metropolitan Palace Hotel

04 227 0000

This stylish, trendy venue is split into two areas: a small, fashionable restaurant serving an interesting selection of international cuisine, and a fabulous chill-out area with comfy seating, low lighting and good music. Top night-time hangout if you're on the Deira side of the creek. Map B 7

Spice Island

Buffet

Renaissance Hotel

04 262 5555

Why try one type of cuisine when you can try 15? That's the somewhat worrying premise behind Spice Island, where the chefs can switch between Italian and Mongolian with apparent ease. Particularly popular with after-work gatherings, Spice Island is always lively – probably helped by the buffet deal that for Dhs. 149 allows you unlimited drinks with your meal. Map B 8

Verre

French

Hilton Dubai Creek

04 227 1111

The food, as you would expect from a Gordon Ramsey restaurant, is fantastic. The decor is simply elegant and the service sublime. And five years since opening it still leaves most of the competition in the shade. Still, in a city overpopulated with very fine restaurants, you may find equally impressive venues with a more vibrant atmosphere. Just don't tell Gordon. Map B 6

Garhoud & Port Saeed

At first glance, Garhoud doesn't appear to be the most dynamic corner of Dubai, but hidden below the surface are some of the city's most popular after-dark haunts.

Al Mijana
Arabic
Le Meridien Dubai
04 282 4040

Al Mijana's delightful setting makes it a great Lebanese option when you're on this side of town. The service is no nonsense and the food similarly standard issue, but as with so many local joints, the freshly baked flat bread makes the difference. Map C 1

Boardwalk
International
Dubai Creek Golf & Yacht Club
04 295 6000

Perched on wooden stilts over the creek, Boardwalk is easily one of the best alfresco venues in the city. From your table on any one of the three wooden decks enjoy the continuous flow of luxury yachts, traditional dhows and motorised abras. Map C 2

Blue Elephant
Thai
Al Bustan Rotana Hotel
04 282 0000

Widely regarded as the best Thai restaurant in town, Blue Elephant offers consistently superb food in a setting so authentic it could be Chiang Mai. The enthusiastic sawadee (Thai welcome) on arrival is a good sign of what's to come, as you sit around the fish-filled indoor lagoon pondering the delicacies. Map C 3

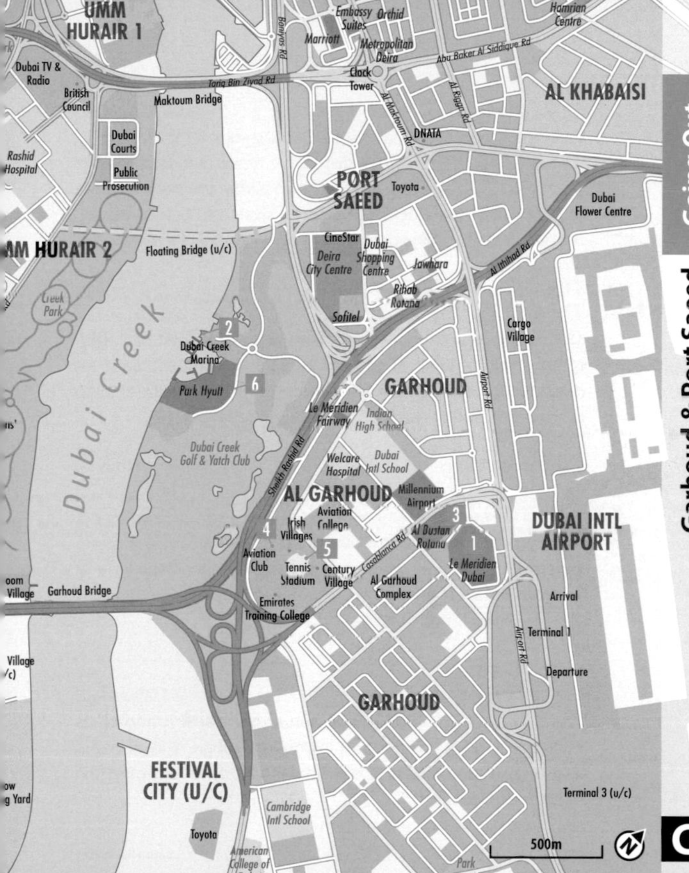
UMM HURAIR 1
Embassy Suites
Orchid
Marriott
Metropolitan Deira
Hamrian Centre
Baniyas Rd
Abu Baker Al Siddique Rd
Dubai TV & Radio
British Council
Tariq Bin Ziyad Rd
Clock Tower
AL KHABAISI
Maktoum Bridge
Al Maktoum Rd
Al Riggat Rd
Dubai Courts
DNATA
Rashid Hospital
Public Prosecution
PORT SAEED
Toyota
Dubai Flower Centre
MM HURAIR 2
Floating Bridge (u/c)
CineStar
Deira City Centre
Dubai Shopping Centre
Jawhara
Al Ittihad Rd
Creek Park
Rihab Rotana
Sofitel
Cargo Village
2
Dubai Creek Marina
Dubai Creek
6
Park Hyatt
GARHOUD
Airport Rd
Le Meridien Fairway
Indian High School
Dubai Creek Golf & Yatch Club
Sheikh Rashid Rd
Welcare Hospital
Dubai Intl School
AL GARHOUD
Millennium Airport
Aviation College
3
Irish Villages
4
Al Bustan Rotana
DUBAI INTL AIRPORT
Casablanca Rd
1
5
Aviation Club
Tennis Stadium
Century Village
Al Garhoud Complex
Le Meridien Dubai
Garhoud Bridge
Arrival
Emirates Training College
Terminal 1
Airport Rd
Departure
GARHOUD
FESTIVAL CITY (U/C)
Cambridge Intl School
Terminal 3 (u/c)
Toyota
American College of Dubai
500m
Park

Cafe Chic

French

Le Meridien Dubai

04 282 4040

Café Chic seems destined to set a Dubai standard for a long time to come. The chef provides distinctive treats before you order your main courses: a small cup of soup before the starter, a taste of pate before the main course, and a sweet trio before dessert. All give a good impression of what lies in wait. Map C 1

The Cellar

Italian

The Aviation Club

04 282 4122

The chapel-style décor of the Cellar makes a pleasant backdrop for the main event: a tantalising wine list and a menu of delicious, modern cuisine. Look out for regular wine-tasting dinners and one of the best brunches in town. Map C 4

Century Village

International

Dubai Tennis Stadium

04 282 4122

This is a microcosm of Dubai's restaurant scene, with a variety of different cuisines packed into a single, cheerful complex. Stand outs include St Tropez, a simple and authentic French bistro, and Sushi, Sushi, a reasonably priced Japanese outlet with excellent all-you-can-eats on Tuesday nights. Map C 5

Irish Village

Pub

The Aviation Club

04 282 4122

Not only does The Irish Village serve the best fish and chips in Dubai, accompanied by an impressive range of cool beers, it also has one of the best outdoor locations for enjoying the black stuff. Map C 4

Clockwise from top left:
Blue Elephant, The Cellar.

Kiku

Japanese

Le Meridien Dubai

04 282 4122

Arguably the best Japanese restaurant in Dubai, Kiku is always packed with Japanese diners and novices looking to expand their range. You have a choice of dining areas, including private tatami rooms, a sushi counter and plain old tables. Map C 1

Long Yin

Chinese

Le Meridien Dubai

04 282 4040

Delicious food and an impressive wine list are Long Yin's specialities. Intimate, classy restaurants rarely come cheap and this is no exception, but the authenticity of both venue and food makes up for the bottom line on your bill. Map C 1

Meridien Village Terrace

Buffet

Le Meridien Dubai

04 282 4040

Offering an alfresco buffet set among tranquil greenery and soothing waterfalls, this place varies its cuisine each night. Sample the exotic dishes from eight live-cooking stations, and drink as much as you can, for a tempting price of Dhs.110. Map C 1

More

Cafe

Le Meridien Dubai

04 282 4040

This chic, minimalist venue is reminiscent of London or Paris. A range of fine comfort food is on offer, with the soup served at your table, highly recommended. A page of the menu is dedicated to coffee, and the fresh-fruit cocktails are superb. Map C 1

M's Beef Bistro

Steakhouse

Le Meridien Dubai

04 282 4040

A heavenly selection of the world's best beef awaits meat lovers at this cosy bistro, with steaks from New Zealand and America sharing top billing. Staff are friendly and will talk you through the menu, which also offers decent vegetarian options. Map C 1

Oxygen

International/Nightclub

Al Bustan Rotana Hotel

04 282 0000

With its opulent interior and incredible deals on drinks (especially for ladies), Oxygen attracts an up-for-it crowd. Punters build up their energy for the dancefloor with a meal from the above average pub grub menu. Map C 3

QD's

Bar

Dubai Creek Golf & Yacht Club

04 295 6000

QD's is a regular late-afternoon hangout of Dubai's cocktail-loving, bright young things, and as the evening wears on it fills up with party people from across the city. Settle into a comfy chair on the banks of the creek and contemplate the ever-changing skyline through a haze of fruity shisha smoke. Map C 2

Rodeo Grill

Steakhouse

Al Bustan Rotana Hotel

04 282 0000

Rodeo Grill's wooden floors and shuttered windows evoke the atmosphere of a gentleman's club, while its stately bar complements the table-side theatrics – be it the mixing of a satisfying Caesar salad or the slicing of a filet for grilling. Guess the weight of the latter correctly and win a free meal. Map C 3

Sukhothai
Thai

Le Meridien Dubai
04 282 4040

With staff dressed in traditional silk costumes and delicious dishes prepared by award-winning Thai chef, Khun Chitlada Thanomsok, this is wonderfully authentic dining. Map C 1

Traiteur
International

Park Hyatt Dubai
04 602 1234

While nine chefs (count 'em) perform in a breathtakingly beautiful kitchen, you descend from an intimate bar via a staircase into a dining room. The performance in the kitchen is matched only by the quality of the food, making this one of Dubai's most prized restaurants. Map C 6

Thai Kitchen
Thai

Park Hyatt Dubai
04 317 2222

Chef Khun Sapatra brings authentic flavors and textures from Thailand's north eastern province of Esarn to bear on his superior range of Thai delicacies. Portions are deliberately small; these are dishes built to share with friends. Map C 6

Yalumba
International

Le Meridien Dubai
04 282 4040

It's billed as modern Australian cooking, but don't expect kangaroo. What you do get is superbly presented and tasty world fusion dining in a classy, New York-style, uptown restaurant. Australia is well represented in the extensive (and expensive) wine list, and the dense, but tasty, range of cheeses. Map C 1

Clockwise from top left: Rodeo Grill, Sukhothai, More.

Jumeira & Satwa

Sho Cho's and its pals at the Dubai Marine Club still pull the weekend crowd despite stiff competition from 'new' Dubai. Satwa's choice of cheap eats, meanwhile, remains unrivalled anywhere in the city.

Al Mallah

Arabic

Al Diyafah Street

04 398 4723

Among the crowd of small Arabic joints in the city, this one stands out. Situated on one of the busiest streets in town, it offers mainly pavement seating with a few tables and chairs inside. The shawarmas and fruit juices are excellent, the cheese and zatar manoushi superb, and the falafel possibly the biggest and best in Dubai. Map D 1

Aussie Legends

Sports Bar

Rydges Plaza Hotel

04 398 2222

Pool tables, TVs showing sport, a smoky atmosphere and subterranean location make Aussie Legends a suitably traditional pub. The surprisingly good bar music adds a bit of spice to the proceedings while the range of pub food is sufficient to soak up the pints. Map D 2

Boudoir

International/Nightclub

Dubai Marine Beach Resort

04 398 5995

This self-proclaimed 'exclusive' nightspot may require a spot of queuing should you arrive after 11:30pm but after fluttering

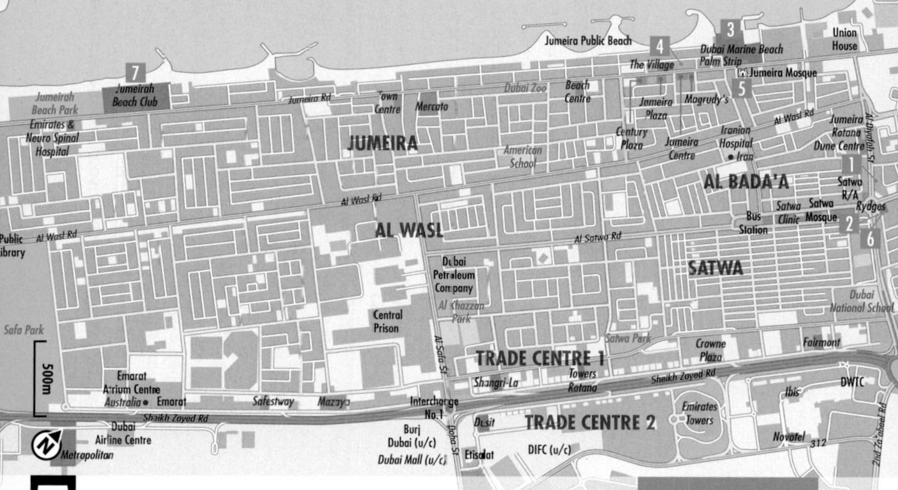

D

Jumeria & Satwa

your eyelids at the bouncer you'll be granted entry to a dimly lit den where a DJ spins the requisite house. Tuesdays and Fridays promise free champagne for ladies and eye-candy for the boys. Map D 3

Cactus Cantina

Tex Mex

Rydges Plaza Hotel 04 398 2274

This is a regular haunt of Dubai's expat population, largely for one reason – the free margaritas for ladies on Thursday evenings. Apart from cheap booze (the rest of the week also offers tempting deals), the hearty food is a firm favourite when you're trying to fend off a hangover. Map D 2

Coconut Grove

Indian

Rydges Plaza Hotel 04 398 3800

If you're after curry in a hurry, then Coconut Grove isn't for you, but if you want to linger over delicious dishes from India, Goa and Sri Lanka then it's ideal. Especially worthy of mention is the ridiciously cheap Friday buffet. The view across this small corner of Dubai is also rather tasty. Map D 2

Il Rustico

Italian

Rydges Plaza Hotel 04 398 2222

Rydges Plaza may seem awkwardly positioned just off Satwa roundabout but this charming, rustic Italian just inside the front doors is worth a look, especially for a lazy lunch. Bare wooden floorboards, beamed ceilings and intimate candlelit tables make for a cosy atmosphere in which diners enjoy a selection of tasty pasta dishes and delicious wood-fired pizzas. Map D 2

Johnny Rockets
American

Opp. Jumeirah Centre
04 344 7859

You'd never have guessed it from the name, but this is a 50s style novelty diner, complete with red vinyl seats, a plastic counter and juke box. The menu of big burgers and fabulous floats will also keep the kids quiet. Happy Days. Map D 4

Lime Tree Café
Cafe

Nr Jumeirah Mosque
04 344 7859

After a hard day's posing on Jumeira beach, why not treat yourself to some of the best deli food in Dubai. The quiches, chunky sandwiches, inventive salads and muffins, cakes and cookies are superb, as are the coffee and the purifying smoothies. Map D 5

Malecon
Cuban

Dubai Marine Resort & Spa
04 346 1111

Malecon's high graffiti-covered walls and low lighting create a sultry Cuban atmosphere, aided by live music and some of Dubai's best Salsa dancers. The menu isn't huge, with the paella your best bet, however, the clientele is pretty tasty. Map D 3

Pars Iranian Kitchen
Iranian

Nr Rydges Plaza
04 398 4000

Don't be put off by the huge neon sign. This is a traditional Arabian restaurant, serving good hummus, moutabel, and tabbouleh, and a selection of grilled meats and kebabs. A delightful front garden, enclosed by a fairy-light-entwined hedgerow, is home to Arabic-cushioned bench seats, perfect for enjoying a leisurely shisha with a group of friends. Map D 6

Prasinos

Mediterranean

Jumeriah Beach Club Resort & Spa — 04 344 5333

While the space at Prasinos is airy, the atmosphere remains intimate, especially on the terrace where stunning views of the exotic gardens and tranquil Arabian Gulf can be enjoyed. The modern Mediterranean menu, which savours seafood, blends traditional fare with inventive dishes. Map D 7

Sho Cho's

Japanese

Dubai Marine Beach Resort & Spa — 04 346 1111

One of a number of party places at the Dubai Marine Beach Resort, Sho Cho's is set around a stunning lagoon close to the shoreline. It may be a Japanese restaurant but the delicate and imaginative dishes are not the real reason that the beautiful people flock here. Come midnight, the DJs take over and the real fun begins. Map D 3

Sidra

Arabic/ Lebanese

Al Diyafah Street — 04 345 3044

In just a short time since opening, Sidra has become one of the most highly rated independent Arabic restaurants in town. Offering dining either inside or out on a terrace overlooking bustling Diyafah Street, it is a great place for inexpensive and excellent Lebanese food. The range of mezze and mains is extensive and includes some unique dishes, all of which are refreshingly light, fresh and clean. Map D 1

Prasinos

New Dubai

What 'new' Dubai lacks in local character it makes up for in luxury cool. From the splendidly self-important Buddha Bar to the awesome array of alfresco options, there's a delicious option on every corner.

Amazeena

Arabic

The Ritz-Carlton

04 399 4000

With a varied and very well-priced selection of Arabic meze, Amazeena is one of the better poolside restaurants in Dubai. Sit back and enjoy dining under the stars or in your own little tent, sampling the shisha while the oud player plucks away in the background. Map E 1

Barasti Bar

Beach Bar

Le Meridien Mina Seyahi

04 393 3333

When you can watch waves lapping at the white sandy shore and sip cocktails under the disappearing sun, it's no wonder that Barasti has had a loyal following for years. Map E 2

The Beach Bar & Grill

Seafood

One&Only Royal Mirage

04 399 9999

After a tranquil walk through the gardens of the One&Only Mirage you reach the Beach Bar & Grill. It's what you'd expect from one of the world's most luxurious hotel chains – tasteful Moroccan decor, imaginative seafood, and a stunning view of the Arabian Gulf. Map E 3

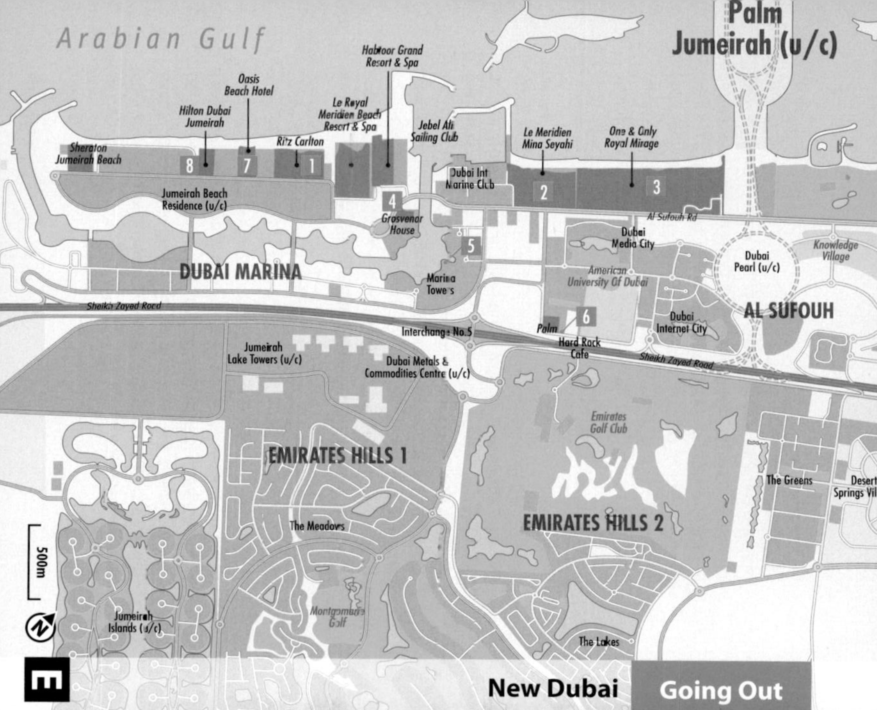

Arabian Gulf
Palm Jumeirah (u/c)
Habtoor Grand Resort & Spa
Oasis Beach Hotel
Le Royal Meridien Beach Resort & Spa
Hilton Dubai Jumeirah
Jebel Ali Sailing Club
Le Meridien Mina Seyahi
One & Only Royal Mirage
Ritz Carlton
Sheraton Jumeirah Beach
8
7
1
2
3
4
5
6
Dubai Int Marine Club
Jumeirah Beach Residence (u/c)
Grosvenor House
Al Sufouh Rd
Dubai Media City
Knowledge Village
Dubai Pearl (u/c)
DUBAI MARINA
Marina Towers
American University Of Dubai
Sheikh Zayed Road
AL SUFOUH
Palm
Dubai Internet City
Interchange No.5
Hard Rock Cafe
Jumeirah Lake Towers (u/c)
Dubai Metals & Commodities Centre (u/c)
Emirates Golf Club
EMIRATES HILLS 1
The Greens
Desert Springs Village
The Meadows
EMIRATES HILLS 2
500m
Jumeirah Islands (u/c)
Montgomerie Golf
The Lakes
E
New Dubai
Going Out

Buddha Bar
Far Eastern

Grosvenor House
04 399 8888

From the entrance, a seductively lit corridor leads you past private lounges and tucked-away alcoves, all perfectly decadent places to dine, lounge and socialise. The grand hall beyond is a feast for the eyes, with its colossal Buddha centrepiece. Not content with one world-class bar, Grosvenor House is also home to the equally luxurious Bar 44 and its stunning view across Dubai Marina. Map E 4

Bussola
Italian

Le Meridien Mina Seyahi
04 399 3333

After a short buggy ride from the hotel to the beach you'll be welcomed at Bussola by helpful staff. The interior is light and airy, with floor-to-ceiling windows meaning you can't help but appreciate the shoreline vistas. Alternatively, the outdoor terrace gets you even closer to the sea. The menu's Sicilian influence means the choices are slightly more adventurous than your standard Italian fare, but delicious nonetheless. Map E 2

Chandelier
Arabic/Lebanese

Marina Walk
04 366 3606

Despite the dodgy name, this place combines decent tunes, chic decor, and nouveau Lebanese cuisine to good effect. Generous portions, with delightful presentation and palate-pleasing flavours, make for an outstanding dining experience. Finish your evening with drinks upstairs in the lounge or shisha on the outdoor waterfront terrace. Map E 5

Clockwise from top: Eau Zone, Bice, Nina.

Eauzone
Far Eastern

One&Only Royal Mirage
04 399 9999

Eauzone's tables, which overlook beautifully lit pools and gardens are in great demand when the weather is good. The menu offers a fusion-style choice of dishes that would tickle the most discerning of taste buds. Map E 3

The Grill Room
Steakhouse

One&Only Royal Mirage
04 399 5533

Cosy and unassuming, this is a great alternative to the big name steakhouses in town. The simple menu offers a range of classic fare, with top quality Australian steaks complemented by perfect potato wedges, all at competitive prices. Map E 3

Hard Rock Café
American

Jct 5, Sheikh Zayed Road
04 399 2888

You know what to expect: big portions of burgers and fries to satisfy the most extreme appetite. Still, when was the Hard Rock experience anything to do with the food? Expect to be dancing with a butch biker come the end of the evening. Map E 6

Indego
Indian

Grosvenor House
04 399 8888

Consultant chef Vineet Bhatia is the only Indian chef in the world with a Michelin star and its not hard to see why. All dishes here are Indian by name, but come with a twist, be it the wild mushroom biryani or the saffron and strawberry Indian tiramisu with cardamon ice cream. Map E 4

Nina

Indian

One&Only Royal Mirage

04 399 9999

Situated within the lavishly furnished Arabian Court, Nina is a firm favourite among visitors to the One&Only Royal Mirage. It's hard to know what's better: the surroundings, service, or the inventive dishes on the modern Indian menu. Map E 3

Oregano

Mediterranean

Oasis Beach Hotel

04 399 4444

The food here is excellent, with an impressive choice of dishes from Italy, France and Spain. Oregano also takes the concept of family feasting seriously enough to offer a separate menu for children. Map E 7

Pachanga

Latin American

Hilton Dubai Jumeriah

04 399 1111

Time for a taste of Latin America in uptown Dubai. Split into Mexican, Argentinian and Brazilian dining areas, Pachanga serves up an extensive range of South American dishes, with a house band and themed salsa and tango nights to spice up proceedings. Map E 8

Rupee Room, The

Indian

Marina Walk

04 390 5755

Occupying a prime spot along the popular Marina Walk, the Rupee Room offers a wide selection of north Indian dishes in relaxed surroundings. Weather permitting, the best tables are outside, and provide spectacular views. With so much in its favour, it's unfortunate that the service can be muddled. Map E 5

Royal Orchid

Thai

Marina Walk

04 399 4000

Royal Orchid offers decent, well-priced Thai and Chinese food in this up and coming part of town. Its waterside dining provides fine views over the marina, while the interior dining area is spread across two spacious floors. Map E 5

Rooftop Lounge & Terrace

Bar

One&Only Royal Mirage

04 399 9999

This bar takes the concept of lounging and relaxation to new levels. With a superb view over Jumeriah Palm, and Dubai's hightest ratio of scatter cushions to customers, this has fast gained a reputation as the place to be seen. Map E 3

Tagine

Moroccan

One&Only Royal Mirage

04 399 9999

Start with the 'pastilla bil hamam' (pigeon pie topped with cinnamon and icing sugar) or any of the other fabulous starters, then indulge in the restaurant's namesake dishes or couscous options. The dessert menu is slightly limited but the excellent 'kenaffa' sums up this excellent Moroccan. Map E 3

The Dhow

Seafood

Le Meridien Mina Seyahi

04 3993333

With its permanent mooring in Dubai Marina and huge variety of excellent seafood, this is one for the big occasion. Choose to dine in the air-conditioned lower deck or go alfresco and enjoy the view of the gulf from above. The variety of fresh oysters, followed by a tantalizing choice of sushi, is superb. Map E 2

Clockwise from top left: Rooftop Lounge & Terrace, Tagine, Pachanga.

Oud Metha & Umm Hurair

Apart from a sprinkling of worthy local eateries, the main draw here is the culinary geography lesson on offer at Wafi City and the plethora of posh spots at the adjacent Grand Hyatt.

Al Koufa

Arabic

Nr Al Nasr Leisureland

04 335 1511

Despite looking like a fake fort and being bigger than a car park, Al Koufa is a solidly performing, popular restaurant and nightspot, especially among locals and Arab expats. There's live music and entertainment, which is recorded for broadcast on a local TV channel, so come 11pm it's packed. Arrive earlier and grab a side table if you're looking for a quieter night. Map F 1

Andiamo!

Italian

Grand Hyatt Dubai

04 317 1234

Brightly coloured furniture and over-sized lava lamps make for a good vibe at this cheerful Italian. The menu features great pizzas, pastas and risottos, light starters and traditional desserts, including excellent homemade gelato. Map F 2

Asha's

Indian

Pyramids

04 324 4100

Love Indian food but bored of the colonial style and subdued decor of most Indian restaurants? Try Asha's. This highly recommended venue – owned by Indian singing legend

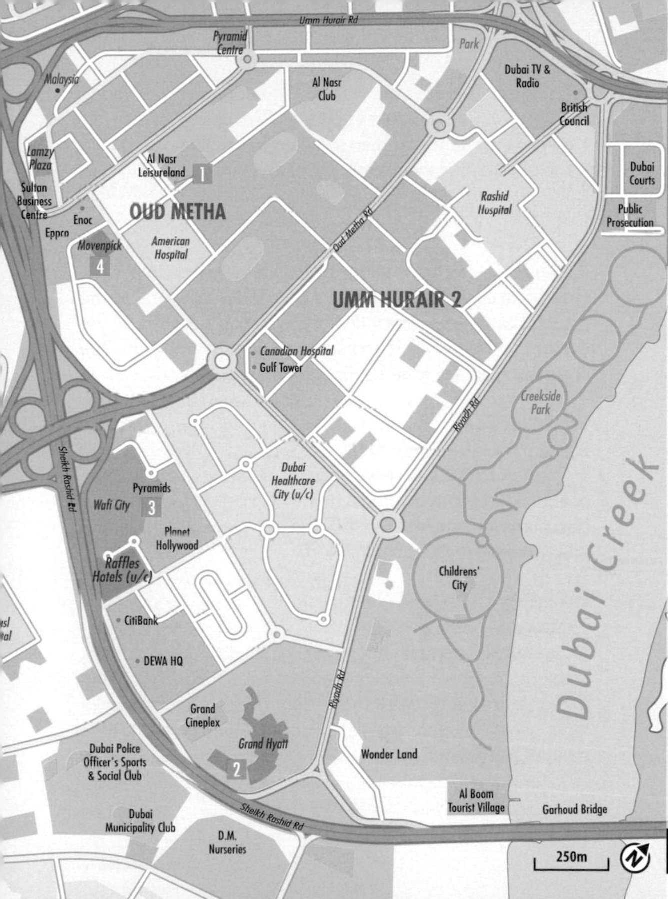

Oud Metha & Umm Hurair

Umm Hurair Rd
Pyramid Centre
Park
Malaysia
Al Nasr Club
Dubai TV & Radio
British Council
Lamzy Plaza
Al Nasr Leisureland
1
Dubai Courts
Sultan Business Centre
OUD METHA
Rashid Hospital
Public Prosecution
Enoc
Eppco
Movenpick
4
American Hospital
Oud Metha Rd
UMM HURAIR 2
Canadian Hospital
Gulf Tower
Creekside Park
Riyadh Rd
Sheikh Rashid Rd
Dubai Healthcare City (u/c)
Pyramids
Wafi City
3
Dubai Creek
Planet Hollywood
Childrens' City
Raffles Hotels (u/c)
CitiBank
DEWA HQ
Riyadh Rd
Grand Cineplex
Grand Hyatt
2
Dubai Police Officer's Sports & Social Club
Wonder Land
Al Boom Tourist Village
Garhoud Bridge
Sheikh Rashid Rd
Dubai Municipality Club
D.M. Nurseries
250m

Asha Bhosle – evokes the vibrancy and enthusiasm of young Mumbai, with its designer interior and snappily dressed staff. The menu offers better-than-standard Indian fare mixed with some of Asha's personal family recipes. Map F 3

Carter's

Bar

Pyramids

04 324 4100

Wicker chairs and old-fashioned ceiling fans create a somewhat cheesy colonial vibe at Carters. As the evening wears on the crowds gather and dance until the wee hours, fuelled by the ever-present drink deals and 80s tunes. For some the epitome of a great night, for others a nightmare scenario. Map F 3

Fakhreldine

Arabic

Movenpick Hotel Bur Dubai

04 336 6000

This top-notch Lebanese venue has it all: an extensive menu, a beautiful interior, live music, a bewitching belly dancer and the best hummus in town. It is easily the best place in Dubai for an unforgettable Arabian night. Map F 4

Ginseng

Asian/Bar

Pyramids

04 248 200

An upmarket cocktail bar, Ginseng, services exotic drinks, fabulous champagne cocktails and an Asian tapas-style menu to carry you through late into the night. Tuesday night is Gemini night, which roughly translated means that if you buy one cocktail, you get one free. Map F 3

Clockwise from top left: Fakhreldine, Indochine, Jimmy Dix.

Indochine

Vietnamese

Grand Hyatt Dubai

04 317 1234

Simple, authentic cuisine rates highly at this popular Vietnamese restaurant. Staff are friendly and efficient, and the set menus, complete with starter, main course, fresh fruit and a selection of teas, are amazingly good value. Map F 2

Jimmy Dix

Nightclub

Movenpick Hotel Bur Dubai

04 336 8800

If sticky floors, smoky air and cheesy pick-up lines are your thing, look no further. You can always count on this friendly bar/ nightclub for a fun-loving crowd and a decent buzz. any night of the week. The dress code is relaxed, so are the bouncers and the live band and DJ keep the crowds happy, especially for the 'Thursday Thump' weekend party. Map F 4

Medzo

Italian

Pyramids

04 324 4100

Medzo is popular with Dubai's city slickers thanks to its classic Mediterranean menu (including a heavenly white chocolate tiramisu), vibrant group of servers and beautiful candle-lit terrace (offering alfresco dining all year round, thanks to outdoor air conditioning). Booking is recommended. Map F 3

Peppercrab

Seafood

Grand Hyatt Dubai

04 317 2222

With an open-plan kitchen and a relaxed atmosphere, Peppercrab offers unpretentious and versatile seafood dining. It's great for a romantic night out, a sophisticated business meal or dinner with a large group of friends. Sadly, the restaurant doesn't quite live up to the hype. When you are paying big bucks for your black pepper crab, you want the dining experience to be extra special. Still, request a seat in the back rooms and you can rip into your (expensive) dinner, and mutter about its cost, in private. Map F 2

Seville's

Spanish

Pyramids

04 3247 300

This is one of the best places in town to unwind, with its terrace perfectly positioned for sundowners. Chilled sangria and a delicious tapas menu hit the spot; the only downside is trying to choose between a selection of hot and cold treats, or the famous Seville's paella. It's always busy at weekends, so reservations are required. In the early evening it's the perfect spot for a candlelit dinner thanks to the live acoustic guitar. Map F 3

Thai Chi

Chinese/Thai

Pyramids

04 3244 100

Two separate kitchens, one Chinese and one Thai, prepare delicious dishes from two of Dubai's most popular cuisines. The relaxed decor of the Chinese room leads into the more formal, luxurious Thai room, but both menus are available, no matter where you sit. Head for the beautiful terrace for dining in cooler months. Map F 3

Sheikh Zayed Road

This is where the hungry hedonists come to play, whether down and dirty in Long's Bar or sleek and sophisticated in the likes of Spectrum on One.

Al Nafoorah
Arabic/Lebanese

Jumeirah Emirates Towers
04 353 680

The classic dishes in this modern Lebanese are served with an inventive twist, with chicken livers, drizzled in pomegranate sauce, highly recommended. Despite its prime location in Emirates Towers, the prices are surprisingly reasonable. Map G 1

Amwaj
Seafood

Shangri-La Hotel
04 343 8888

This seafood restaurant is everything you might expect from the Shangri-La. The decor is modern and understated, as is the service, while the menu offers an imaginative range of dishes, predominantly, but not exclusively, seafood. Map G 2

Blue Bar
Jazz Bar

Novotel World Trade Centre
04 332 0000

The jazz is smooth, the decor silky and the atmosphere sultry in this understated glass/chrome bar. Visit on a Thursday night to catch local musicians jamming, otherwise, sit back and let the DJ do the work, while you savour a selection of Belgium's finest draft and bottled beers. Map G 3

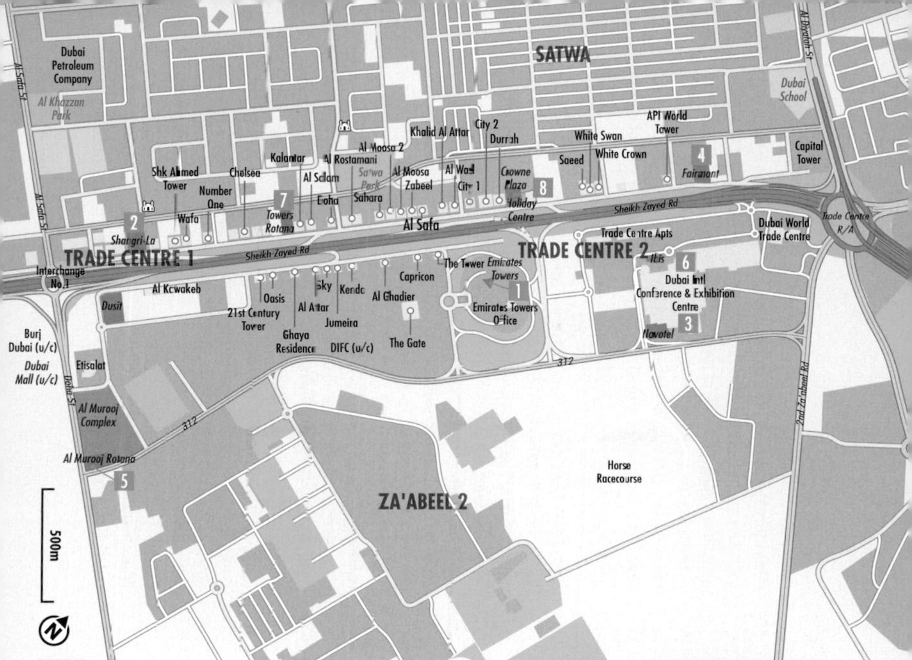

SATWA
Dubai Petroleum Company
Al Khazzan Park
Al Safa St
Dubai School
Al Diyafah St
API World Tower
Capital Tower
4
Fairmont
White Swan
White Crown
Saeed
City 2
Durrah
Khalid Al Attar
Al Moosa 2
Al Rostamani
Kalantar
Shk Ahmed Tower
Chelsea
Number One
Al Salam
Satwa Park
Al Moosa
Zabeel
Al Wasl
City 1
Crowne Plaza
8
Holiday Centre
Doha
Sahara
7
Towers Rotana
Wafa
2
Shangri-La
Al Safa
Sheikh Zayed Rd
TRADE CENTRE 1
TRADE CENTRE 2
Trade Centre Apts
Dubai World Trade Centre
Trade Centre R/A
Ibis
6
Dubai Intl Conference & Exhibition Centre
3
Novotel
Interchange No.1
Al Kawakeb
Dusit
Oasis
21st Century Tower
Sky
Kendo
Al Attar
Ghaya Residence
Jumeira
DIFC (u/c)
Al Ghadier
Capricon
The Gate
The Tower
Emirates Towers
1
Emirates Towers Office
312
Burj Dubai (u/c)
Dubai Mall (u/c)
Etisalat
Doha St
Al Murooj Complex
Al Murooj Rotana
5
ZA'ABEEL 2
Horse Racecourse
2nd Za'abeel Rd
500m
N
G

Cin Cin

Bar

The Fairmont Dubai

04 311 8000

This intimate wine bar is surprisingly spacious but has a sufficient number of hideaways should you want a private aperitif or a cosy late-night tipple. The long bar is backed by a wall stacked with wine to make even the most snooty vin buff pause in awe. As the clock ticks towards midnight, the clientele starts to bring a bit of life to the stark surrounds, and the bar bills rise accordingly. Map G 4

Double Decker

Pub

Al Murooj Rotana Hotel

04 321 1111

A pub themed around London Transport you say? Cramped, sticky and ultimately disappointing? Not a bit of it. An adventurous cocktail menu is complemented by a comprehensive and informative wine list, and the upmarket pub food covers a broad range of tasty snacks and meals. Map G 5

Lotus One

Thai/Bar

Dubai Intl Convention Centre

04 405 2704

With its attempt at Phillipe Starck, glass split-level floors, inventive fabric partitions and uber-cool lighting, Lotus One is laying its claim for the coolest place to dine in Dubai. The food, fusing Thai, Vietnamese and Korean, is nothing but hip. Map G 6

Mosaico

Italian

Dubai Intl Convention Centre

04 319 8088

This stylish and relaxed Italian venue boasts an intimate terrace and the largest mosaic in the Middle East. The menu offers a good choice, especially for vegetarians. It's especially good for spontaneous (post-club) dining as the kitchen is open 24 hours. Map G 6

Marrakech

Moroccan

Shangri-La Hotel

04 343 8888

Moroccan food may be a little under-represented in Dubai but the rather swish Marrakech proves there's a gap in the market for this cuisine. Salads and perfectly light bastilla make way for the hearty, rich tagines and couscous dishes. Map G 2

The Noodle House

Far Eastern

Jumeirah Emirates Towers

04 319 8088

Just turn up and wait for the first available spot at one of the long communal tables, then order by ticking your desired dishes on the pads provided (after some advice from the friendly, clued-up staff if required). The Far Eastern food is as unfussy as the service. Map G 1

The Rib Room

Steakhouses

Jumeirah Emirates Towers

04 319 8768

As you would expect from an Emirates Towers restaurant, The Rib Room is cool, sharp and smooth. This is a relatively large, open place but low lighting means it retains a certain intimacy. If you don't fancy the mainly carnivorous menu (surely Rib Room was a clue?) then vegetarian options are also available. Map G 1

Scarlett's

American
Jumeirah Emirates Towers
04 319 8768

Scarlett's remains a decent party place despite tough competition. The restaurant does feel a bit like a wedding reception where the tables and chairs have been hastily arranged to overlook the dance floor, but it's a great place for big groups who want to eat, drink and be merry. The commercial dance music, drunk businessmen and plumes of cigarette smoke might scupper a family gathering. Map G 1

Shang Palace

Chinese
Shangri-La Hotel
04 343 8888

Choose to people-watch from the balcony overlooking the Shangri La's bustling lobby, or take a quieter position inside the circular dining room. Shang's menu is extensive when compared with its city rivals – shark fin soup, live seafood, dim sum and then some should you be peckish. Map G 2

Spectrum on One

International
The Fairmont Dubai
04 311 8000

Each corner of the culinary world has found its own space in this modern, impeccably designed restaurant, where you are invited to 'Taste a Nation'. Enjoy an aperitif in the cosy bar and whet your appetite by slowly digesting the menu, or plough into a decent bottle of red from the impressive open cellar. Map G 4

Clockwise from top left: Blue Bar, Double Decker, Tokyo @ the Towers.

tokyo@the towers

Japanese

Jumeirah Emirates Towers

04 319 8088

The star of this show is definitely the teppanyaki, which features a range of soup and salad starters followed by delicious seafood, beef or chicken cooked in front of you by a skilful and charismatic chef. For desert there's a spot of light embarrassment at the adjacent karaoke bar. Map G 1

Teatro

Japanese

Towers Rotana Hotel

04 343 8000

The open sushi kitchen that greets you as you enter Teatro is just the start of the global culinary journey that awaits. A true fusion of cultures and tastes, the menu is a mix of Japanese, Chinese, Indian and European. Beware the ice-cold air con. Map G 7

Trader Vic's

Polynesian/Cocktail Lounge

Crowne Plaza

04 331 1111

Something of an institution, mainly for its cosy bar where the cocktail menu entices a party crowd, Trader Vic's offers punters some potent concoctions. The restaurant's Polynesian menu is tempting should you still be standing. Map G 8

Vu's Bar

Bar

Jumeirah Emirates Towers

04 319 8088

The views across Dubai's sprawling metropolis from this 51st-floor bar are not to be missed. Vu's isn't cheap, but for sophisticated sundowners and showing off to out-of-towners it takes some beating. Map G 1

Vu's Restaurant

Mediterranean

Jumeirah Emirates Towers

04 319 8088

More than living up to its name, with an unobstructed panorama of the city from every table, Vu's is the highest restaurant (for now) in the Middle East. The menu is dominated by modern European cuisine, and its standouts include caviar linguine and the signature dishes of lobster and roast pigeon. Map G 1

Wagamama

Japanese

Crowne Plaza

04 305 6060

Modelled on the traditional Japanese ramen bar, Wagamama's contemporary, stream-line design works well for a quick bite or a more leisurely dining experience. Orders are taken and electronically sent directly to the kitchen where they are immediately and freshly prepared. The menu is extensive and covers a wide variety of noodle and rice dishes, all of which are generously served. Map G 8

Zaika

Indian

Al Murooj Rotana

04 321 1111

Spread across two floors, Zaika has private rooms on the mezzanine floor and a classic and relaxed dining space on the ground level. The dishes stay true to the ancient methods of Indian cooking, using the flavours and styles that have made this one of the world's most popular cuisines. Map G 5

Umm Suqeim

Just next door to the Burj Al Arab is the Souk Madinat Jumeirah, a huge two-hotel resort with a wide variety of cosmopolitan outlets hidden in its Arabic-styled labyrinth.

360° — Bar

Jumeirah Beach Hotel — 04 348 000

One of two much-hyped bars in the ever-popular Jumeriah Beach Hotel, 360 lives up to its billing. It's hard not to be blown away by the views of the Gulf from its deck and that's before we get to the beanbags, satisfying Shisha and stylish sundowners. Map H 1

The Agency — Bar

Souk Madinat Jumeirah — 04 366 6335

Smart, slick and sharp, this modern bar is at the stylish end of the outlets hidden away in the Arab-esque Souk Madinat. Like its nearby rivals, there is an ever-present terrace where you can enjoy the impressive wine list and sample the small (but adequate) tapas. Map H 6

Al Mahara — Seafood

Burj Al Arab — 04 301 7600

Dining at Al Mahara begins with a simulated submarine ride that plunges you into a marine-themed wonderland (this is Dubai, remember). The menu then offers some exciting seafood creations – opt for the sampler, or traditional a la carte. Map H 2

Arabian Gulf
2
Burj Al Arab
5
Al Qasr
4
Mina A' Salam
1
Jumeirah Beach Hotel
Wild Wadi Water Park
Souk Madinat Jumeirah
6
Umm Suqeim Beach
Umm Suqeim Park
e-Library
Health Centre
Jumeira Rd
Al Thanya Rd
Al Manara Rd
UMM SUQEIM 3
UMM SUQEIM 2
Kings Dubai School
AL SUFOUH
Umm Suqeim Rd
Al Wasl Rd
Dubai Police Academy
Dubai TV Relay Station
AL MANARA
UMM AL SHEIF
Emirates International School
Sheikh Zayed Road
Interchange No 4
Interchange No 3
Kempinski
3
Mall of the Emirates
Tasjeel
Bur Dubai Traffic Dept
Gold & Diamond Park
Gold & Diamond Museum
500m
Dubai American Academy
323 Rd
AL QUOZ IND AREA 3
AL QUOZ IND AREA 1
H

Aprés

International/Bar

Mall of the Emirates

04 3412575

Complete with a cosy fireplace, this ski lodge-cum-restaurant offers good wholesome fare including steaks and pasta – perfect for replenishment after a hard day on the (fake) slopes. Share the fondue for that authentic Alps experience. Map H 3

Bahri Bar

Bar

Mina A'Salam

04 366 8888

Imagine you had the chance to design the perfect bar. For starters you'd include a stunning view, say, windtower rooftops, with the towering Burj Al Arab and sparkling ocean beyond. The bar itself could perhaps have rich furnishings, and intimate lighting both inside and out. On the menu you'd include a comprehensive cocktail selection and delicious nibbles including Arabic hot and cold mezze and tapas. Yep, someone got there first. It's at Mina A'Salam and it's called Bahri Bar. Map H 4

Barzar

International/Bar

Al Qasr Hotel

04 366 8888

Barzar is a funky split-level bar boasting a terrace that overlooks the spectacular Madinat lagoon and the impressive Mina A'Salam hotels. While so many venues in Dubai attempt to be all things to all people, Barzar sticks to being a solidly reliable bar, albeit one with very famous beer cocktails. Map H 5

Al Mahara

Beachcombers
Far Eastern

Jumeirah Beach Hotel
04 406 8999

Located right on the beach, with fantastic views of Burj Al Arab, this bedecked, breezy seaside shack hosts atmospheric Far Eastern buffets every night. A good range of stir-fry, noodle and Peking duck, curry hot pots and satay stalls offer great variety, and there's plenty more to chose from in the starter and seafood salad section. The food's good and staff attentive, but the biggest selling-point is its location. Map H 1

Dhow & Anchor
Pub

Jumeirah Beach Hotel
04 406 8999

If you have to go to a pub while on holiday then at least make it one with a spacious terrace and splendid views of Burj Al Arab. For an added bonus, the menu offers a diverse choice of salads, curries, seafood, meat, sandwiches and simple, well-executed desserts. The wine list is worthy of a fine dining venue, while the service is courteous and relaxed. Map H 1

Jambase
Cajun

Souk Madinat Jumeirah
04 366 8888

Like many of the venues within the Madinat, Jambase is a hedonistic hideaway. Offering nouveau Cajun dining from a limited yet exquisite menu, what it lacks in variety it makes up for in creativity. Complemented by a good cocktail selection and the subdued sounds of a blues/jazz band in the evening, this is well worth seeking out. Map H 6

Koubba

Bar

Al Qasr Hotel

04 366 8888

A stunning venue, both inside and out, where you can languish in regal luxury with the finest views of the Madinat's sprawling resort. Outside, the dome-topped terrace offers a panorama over the waterways, gardens, pool and beach. Inside, the beautifully decorated rustic stone-walled lounge encourages lingering over delicious cocktails. Map H 5

Left Bank

Bar

Souk Madinat Jumeirah

04 366 8888

This is stylish yet informal and a perfect place for a long lunch, aperitif or casual evening meal. You can sample something from the cosmopolitan menu in the lounge-style ultra-modern interior, or enjoy sundowners on the terrace with spectacular waterfront views. There's also a five-minute theatre menu to ensure you don't miss 'curtains up' at the Madinat Theatre. Map H 6

Marina Seafood Market

Seafood

Souk Madinat Jumeirah

04 406 8181

Taking the golf buggy down the jetty towards this excellent seafood restaurant is part and parcel of a uniquely luxurious experience. Fish, oysters and giant shrimp are displayed on ice as well as in tanks, which are also home to chunky lobsters. The menu also incorporates chicken, steak, duck and quail but the best option is the fish market, where you select the fresh ingredients for your meal, and then have it cooked to your liking. Map H 6

Clockwise from top left: Zheng He's, Trilogy, The Wharf.

Pierchic

Seafood

Al Qasr Hotel

04 366 8888

The food is first class, with not one detail left unattended, the service is amiable if not a little too relaxed, and the extensive wine would satisfy most connoisseurs, but it's Pierchic's fantastic location that sets it apart. A five-minute stroll across a wooden pier, with a breathtaking and unobstructed view of the Burj Al Arab, leads you to a rustic restaurant which atop wooden stilts and lit in glorious turquoise from beneath the water. Map H 5

Sahn Eddar

Afternoon Tea

Burj Al Arab

04 301 7777

From the lavish interior of the Burj to the enticing shores of the Arabian Gulf, the views from this decadent venue are unforgettable. You can order from the à la carte menu or sample the formidable afternoon tea. Sit back, relax and be treated like aristocracy as personable staff serve up a feast of sweets, sandwiches, scones, and a pot of fragrant tea or coffee. Map H 2

Shoo Fee Ma Fee

Moroccan

Souk Madinat Jumeirah

04 366 6335

Fine Moroccan food is served in the elegantly appointed interior or on the terrace with wonderful views across the Madinat's waterways. More importantly, Shoo Fee Ma Fee is one of the few restaurants in Dubai where you can choose between roasted goat leg and camel kofta. Map H 6

Trilogy

Nightclub

Souk Madinat Jumeirah 04 366 8888

Taking its name from the number of floors, Trilogy brings the super-club concept to Dubai. There are six bars to choose from, as well as private lounges. For a truly decadent but mildly unnerving experience, treat yourself to a VIP glass cage on the second level and peer down on the action below. Map H 6

Uptown

International

Jumeirah Beach Hotel 04 406 8181

Take the elevator to the 24th floor to find this small but perfectly formed bar. The cool interior is classy enough, but Uptown's USP is the outdoor terrace – it's a perfect spot for 'sunset behind the Burj' photo opportunities. Get there at 6pm sharp for the half-price happy hour. Map H 1

Villa Beach Restaurant

International

Souk Madinat Jumeirah 04 406 8999

Follow the signs for one of Dubai's most isolated restaurants and you'll be greeted by a spectacular view of the Burj and its changing colours. Don't miss the lobster starter but remember to go slow and savour the Mediterranean mains. Map H 6

Zheng He's

Chinese

Souk Madinat Jumeirah 04 366 8888

With its contemporary take on classic dishes and waterside terrace this is one of the highlights of the Madinat. The menu is varied, if a little mystifying, but the food lives up to the sumptuous surroundings. Map H 6

Bahri Bar

Visitor info

Visas and customs

While the UAE is a welcoming nation, its visa requirements vary for different nationalities and also have a tendency to change, so check before you travel.

All travellers, except those carrying a passport from the Arab Gulf Co-operation Council (GCC states), need a visa, but the majority of nationalities automatically get a visit visa stamp in their passport upon arrival, and in most cases it will be valid for 60 days. For some nationalities, a visa must be obtained from a local entity, like a hotel or tour operator, at a cost of Dhs.100 and is only valid for 30 days (and is most likely to be non-renewable).

The good news is that there are two reception services available to help travellers with visa formalities and also bypass the queues. Marhaba Service (04 224 5780) will greet and guide you through immigration and baggage collection if you book with them at least 24 hours in advance. It usually costs Dhs.75 for one passenger from immigration and Dhs.150 per person from the aircraft door. Ahlan Dubai (04 216 5030) is more of a customer service and information department, but they will still assist with visa delivery and customer queries.

Checking your luggage

There are no custom duties levied for personal belongings coming into the country and the customs department is pretty straightforward. Once you've collected your belongings they are x-rayed before you leave, and it's here that magazines, books, videos and DVDs are checked (as long as the media isn't lewd, there won't be a problem). Pornography (and obviously drugs) are illegal. Although the UAE has a more relaxed policy on prescription drugs than many other countries, certain medications (such as codeine) are banned, even though they may be widely available over the counter in other countries. It is a criminal offence to bring them into the country, so it's always best to check with your embassy in advance if you have prescription medication.

There are currently no restrictions on the import/export of local or foreign currency, however the limit for undeclared cash is Dhs.40,000.

Once you're out of the airport, there are 12 car rental companies and an airport shuttle service which takes you into the city. Alternatively, there are plenty of taxis to take you to your hotel. An average taxi fare will cost Dhs.40 to the creek and between Dhs.60-70 to the beach. There is an automatic starting fee of Dhs.20 from the airport.

Airport

Dubai airport is fabulously modern and very easy to navigate. It's said that you ought to be off the plane and out of the airport in 12 and a half minutes. And while it's impossible to guarantee that kind of speed, it's fair to say that as long as you adhere to the rules, you'll fly through the concourse and out into the city in no time.

Duty free allowances:

- **Cigarettes – 2,000**
- **Cigars – 400**
- **Tobacco – 2 kg**
- **Alcohol - (non-Muslim adults only – two litres of spirits and two litres of wine)**

Travel essentials

A few practical things you should know about the city hoping to attract 15 million tourists a year by 2010.

Health requirements

Unless you have recently been in an area where you could have been exposed to cholera or yellow fever, there is no need to get a health certificate before you enter Dubai. Restrictions can change though, so it is better to check health requirements before you travel (see the World Health Organisation website www.who.int/ith/en). There is no risk of getting malaria in the city of Dubai. However, be aware that the malaria-carrying mosquito has on rare occasions been encountered in the mountain and wadi areas of the UAE.

Travel insurance

If you're travelling anywhere in the world, you should always get travel insurance. Choose a reputable insurer and take your time to pick a plan that will suit the activities you intend to enjoy in Dubai, especially if they involve extreme sports such as quad biking or diving.

Female visitors

The UAE is incredibly progressive in comparison to its neighbours. Women are as free here as anywhere else in the Western world – well, almost. In terms of hassle, men stare a lot, especially on public beaches. In such situations, it's better to ignore it and save yourself any aggravation. It also helps to avoid excessively tight or revealing clothing. Dubai Police are very helpful and happy to deal with unwanted attention and hassle.

Disabled visitors

Many of the hotels here are wheelchair enabled as is the Dubai International Airport, but that's unfortunately where it ends because facilities for disabled visitors are limited, particularly at tourist attractions. Always ask if somewhere has wheelchair access and be sure to get specific explanations since an escalator is considered 'wheelchair access' to some.

Time, business and social hours

The local time here is +4hrs UCT (Universal Co-ordinated Time, formerly GMT) with no summer saving time and therefore no clocks changing. This doesn't, of course, correlate with the rest of the world and its time saving methods. Life here starts when the sun sets and the weather has cooled down a bit; evenings and late nights being the best time to see Dubai in full bustle.

Currency

Local currency is the 'Dirham' (Dhs), also referred to as AED (Arab Emirate Dirham), and has been tied to the US dollar since the end of 1980. One Dirham is made up of100 'fils' and coin denominations are Dhs.1, 50 fils, 25 fils, 10 fils and 5 fils, though the last two are rare, and more often than not you won't be getting exact change back. Denominations come in Dhs.5, 10, 20, 50, 100, 200, 500 and 1,000 notes.

Photography

Don't walk around happily snapping random people without asking permission first, particularly women, as it's considered offensive and disrespectful. So be polite, ask first – or simply refrain. Also be careful at which building you're pointing your lens, since government buildings, military installations, ports and airports are not allowed to be photographed.

Go mobile

The Dhs.90 Ahlan package gives you a local phone number for 90 days and can be picked up at the Etisalat Kiosk at Dubai Airport. The first three-minute international call, 90 minutes of local talk time and nine national or international SMS messages are free. If you are calling a local number from an international mobile you will have to dial the city code first (04 for Dubai) and 050 or 055 if you're calling a mobile. See the pull-out map for more dialling codes.

Banks and ATMs

There is a massive network of local and international banks, strictly controlled by the UAE Central Bank, offering a full range of banking services. Normal banking hours are Saturday to Wednesday 08:00 – 13:00 (some also open 16:30 – 18:30) and on Thursday 08:00 – 12:00. ATMs are available at every bank and will accept almost every card. Most shopping centres and hotels will also have ATM machines and you can even find the odd one at a petrol station. For non-UAE based cards, the exchange rates used in the transaction are usually extremely competitive.

In an emergency

Tourist police: Without a doubt, Dubai is one of the safest places in the world but that doesn't mean that accidents – and crimes – don't happen. Lucky then that the Dubai Police (800 4438) have set up a special Department for Tourist Security to better serve the city's visitors.

Lost and stolen property: You will be pleasantly surprised at the abundance of honest people here and it's not unusual for missing valuables, dropped wallets or forgotten credit cards to be handed in. But if you're still unlucky then call either Dubai Police or the Tourist Police to report your valuables lost or stolen. When it comes to your travel documents, paperwork or passport, do the smart thing and leave photocopies with friends.

Hospitals and healthcare: The standard of healthcare is very good whether you opt for a private or government-run hospital. For a list of hospitals, see the pull-out map.

Car accidents: While the infrastructure is superb, the general standard of driving is not. Traffic accidents are plentiful and rubbernecking (drivers slowing down to have a good gawp) is rife. Should you find yourself in such an unfortunate situation, get everyone to safety, call the police and await their instructions.

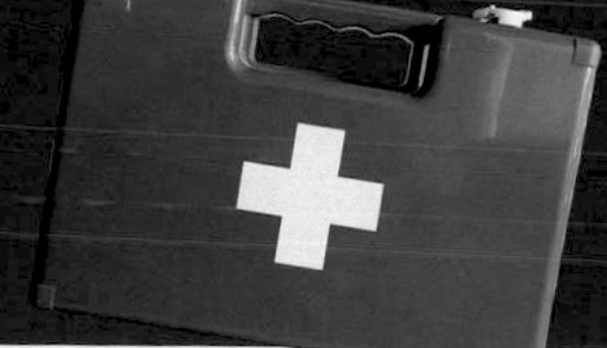

Getting around

Dubai's transport options are surprisingly effective considering the city is in the middle of the desert. Just don't expect to stroll too far, especially in the summer.

Taxi

The majority of taxis are metered and operate under four private companies, and can be flagged down by the side of the road or called on 04 208 0808. Pick-up fare is either Dhs.3 or Dhs.3.50, depending on the time of day or taxi company. Taxis are by far the most common way to get around in Dubai.

Car hire

Despite the questionable driving habits of folks here, renting a car is a good way to get around – as long as you've got the stomach for the haphazard roads. All the leading rental companies have an office in Dubai, plus there's a few good local options, so it's best to shop around for a good rate. Check whether the price includes comprehensive insurance.

Bus

It's not an urban myth. Dubai Municipality's Transport Section does actually operate around 59 bus routes for the emirate, serving the main residential and commercial areas, with new routes coming soon. Fares are cheap (between Dhs.1–3 per journey) and paid to the driver as you board. It's not how most visitors choose to get around, but it is a viable option.

Boat
Dhows (traditional, low wooden boats locally known as abras) are the ultimate way to experience 'old' Dubai. Crossing the creek is actually easier this way and incredibly cheap. For a little bit more money you can take a 12-hour boat ride to Iran from Dubai or Sharjah.

Walking
Dubai is not pedestrianised, so don't expect many brisk walks to the local store. And even if you wanted to defy the concrete city, the sweltering heat will have you reaching for an air-conditioned cab in no time – trust us on this one. Come the winter it's a different story, with many people taking to the few sidewalks (mainly by the creek in Deira and a few spots in Jumeira) for an evening stroll.

Cycling
It's do-able, but drivers are ruthless and extra care should be taken. There are no dedicated cycle lanes, apart from a 1.2km cycling track along Al Mumzar Corniche (which should take all of six minutes to cover).

Car rental agencies

Autolease rent-a-car	04 282 6565
Avis Rent a Car	04 295 7121
Budget Rent-A-Car	04 295 6667
Diamond Lease	04 343 4300
Hertz Rent A Car	04 282 4442
National Car Rental	04 335 5447
Thrifty	04 800 4694
United Car Rentals	04 266 6286

Annual events

Whether you want to witness the world's most expensive horse race, watch Roger Federer in action, or simply shop for two months solid, this is the place to do it.

Dubai Desert Classic — January

www.dubaidesertclassic.com

Where else will you see the masterful swing of Tiger Woods with the desert as a backdrop? If you already know your bunkers from your birdies then you may be aware of Dubai's growing reputation in the golfing world. Alongside the city's inspired and awesomely designed courses, this event helps secure Dubai's status in the game. Sanctioned by the PGA European Tour, the tournament regularly draws the game's biggest names to Dubai's warm shores.

Dubai Tennis Open — February

www.dubaitennischampionships.com

Roger Federer, Andre Agassi and the Williams sisters have all grunted their way around Dubai Tennis Stadium in an attempt to win the US$1 million cash prize at this Tier II WTA and ATP International Series event. Whether or not you're into tennis, this tournament is worth your while – it's always highly entertaining, and you don't have to queue for nine hours to get tickets (Wimbledon, take note). For an extra incentive, the stadium is next door to the Irish Village pub, making the wait between matches refreshingly more entertaining.

SAP
VICTORY
TEAM
DUBAI-UAE
SUPERFUND
77

Dubai International Jazz Festival
March

www.chilloutproductions.com

Get yourself a beanbag and a ticket for one of the coolest events of the year. Since its inception four years ago, this musical extravaganza has been a winner, not only matching but far exceeding expectations. Top-name artists and bands from around the world take to the stage at the pretty Media City Park over three days and nights spreading good vibes to over 18,000 music lovers.

Dubai World Cup
March

www.dubaiworldcup.com

This is an absolute must for your diary. Get your glad rags on and tip your good hat forward for a see-and-be-seen night at the races. This is the world's richest horse race, where thoroughbreds, riders and horse owners compete for the incredible US$6million jackpot.

Camel Racing
From October

www.nadalshebaclub.com

Having rid itself of bad press over its use of child jockeys (don't worry, they use robots now), camel racing goes from strength to strength in Dubai. And when you think that these ungainly creatures can change hands for as much as Dhs. 10 million, it's no wonder that everybody gets so excited. Morning races take place throughout the year at Nad Al Sheba and start very early. You need to be there by 7:00 as the races are over by 8:30. Admission is free.

Dubai Rugby Sevens — November

www.dubairugby7s.com

World-class rugby and the odd bucket of beer fuel the frenzy at this well-established and much-loved sporting event. The games are the official starting point of the IRB Sevens World Series, and whether you're into rugby or not, it is well worth your weekend. It's all rounded off with 'Rugby Rock', a gig by an (as yet unnamed) international band.

Dubai International Film Festival — December

www.dubaifilmfest.com

This festival is still in its infancy but it's already making big waves in the film world. It helps of course that the organizers schmooze the right people at Cannes and are able to attract stars such as Morgan Freeman and Orlando Bloom. A must for fans of every genre, from action to art-house.

Dubai Shopping Festival (DSF) — January-February

It's every shopaholics fantasy – for two whole months Dubai turns into a mammoth bargain bucket. DSF, as it's more commonly known, is far more than a retail extravaganza, with great entertainment and events being held across the city.

Dubai Summer Surprises — June-September

www.mydsf.com

Summer Surprises is similar to DSF but run on a slightly smaller scale. Initially a ploy to entice more people to the city during the blisteringly hot summer months, it's grown to be a big hit among families who want to keep their kids entertained.

Places to stay

Looking for a youth hostel? You're in luck. There is one. For everyone else, there's a choice of hotels, from the spectacular to the downright extravagant. Then, of course, there's the Burj...

While there is budget accommodation in Dubai, most visitors aren't too interested in roughing it. And would you when this city has the greatest concentration of five-star hotels anywhere in the world. Despite a new one rising from the sands every week, there's no sign of saturation. In fact occupancy levels remain consistently high, and demand can even outstrip supply in the cooler winter months.

This could have something to do with their ludicrous luxury and superb facilities, or it could be because Dubai's hotels also play host to the city's thriving restaurant and bar scene. Nearly all licensed restaurants and bars are found in hotels, which means you get to sample all the best bits without having to change rooms. Dubai's hotels tend to be found by the beach, the creek or in the city. But wherever you're staying you'll only be a short taxi ride from another spectacular spa or sundowner.

Should your budget stretch, it's also worth considering a few nights at a desert resort such as Bab Al Shams (p.241). Of course you've probably made your decision – five nights at the Burj Al Arab and the credit card bill from hell.

Al Bustan Rotana Hotel

www.rotana.com 04 282 0000

With 50 comfortable rooms and suites and a wide range of leisure facilities, this hotel is ideal for a weekend break. It has lush gardens which attract a fantastic range of local flora and fauna. There are two pools, two floodlit tennis courts and a volleyball court, as well as a fitness centre and children's playground.

Al Murooj Rotana

www.rotana.com 04 321 1111

Offering a range of accommodation for guests staying short and long-term, Al Murooj is within easy reach of the central trade centre area. There are good leisure facilities including two swimming pools, and the ten restaurant and bars include the excellent Indian restaurant, Zaika, and one of the city's most popular pubs, Double Decker.

Burj Al Arab

www.burj-al-arab.com 04 301 7777

Resembling a billowing sail, the world's tallest hotel stands on its own man-made island, and is as dramatic as it lavish and exclusive, with guests looked after by a host of eager butlers. Non-guests can try afternoon tea at Sahn Eddar (Dhs.190) or a drinks package at Sky View Bar (Dhs.200 for two drinks and canapés).

Coral Deira Hotel

www.coral-deira.com 04 224 8587

The interior of this hotel was designed by legendary Italian firm, Saporiti, so no wonder it promotes itself as a five-star boutique property. Business travellers are served well by its location in the heart of Deira's business district. For those with more cultural pursuits in mind, it is just a short stroll from the gold and spice souks.

Crowne Plaza

www.dubai.crowneplaza.com 04 331 1111

Situated in the buzzing hub of Dubai, this complex has its own shopping mall, as well a Nautilus Health Club, not to mention 12 bars, restaurants and cafes including Trader Vic's for great cocktails and Polynesian food, and Wagamama, the trendy noodle bar chain. There's also Zinc, a Dubai club worth queuing for.

Dubai Marine Beach Resort and Spa

www.dxmarine.com 04 346 1111

The only beach hotel close to the centre of Dubai, this independent property has 195 villa-style rooms nestled among lush, green landscaped gardens, waterfalls and streams. There are three swimming pools, a spa, and a small private beach. Its wide variety of restaurants and bars are perennially popular, especially Sho Cho's.

Dusit Dubai

www.dusit.com 04 343 3333

The building might look like a giant pair of trousers but it actually represents a pair of hands with palms pressed together in a traditional Thai greeting. Restaurants and bars include Champagne Lounge and Benjarong – the hotel's signature Thai restaurant. Situated on Sheikh Zayed Road, the hotel has 321 rooms, suites and one and two-bedroom serviced apartments.

Emirates Towers Hotel

www.jumeriah.com 04 330 0000

The 305 metres that make up this ultra-modern complex include 400 luxury rooms and suites, two floors of high-end fashion outlets and superb dining. It's currently standing as the third tallest building in the world and the tallest in the Middle East and Europe, hence the views of the city from Vu's Bar on the 51st floor are not to be missed.

Fairmont Dubai

www.fairmont.com 04 332 5555

All work and no play makes for very dull Dubai visitors, so we're grateful for the Canadian chain, Fairmont. Their hotel, situated in the heart of the city on Sheikh Zayed Road, gives any holiday a kick-start. From intriguing décor and amazing eateries to one of the trendiest nightclubs in town, the Fairmont does a good job of pleasing everyone.

Grand Hyatt Dubai

www.dubai.grand.hyatt.com 04 317 1234

Touted as Dubai's major luxury conference and leisure hotel, this resort takes up a massive 37 acres of prime creek-side location. Everything here is geared towards the business traveller with all 674 luxury rooms and suites kitted out with the latest gadgets. There are also furnished and unfurnished apartments for longer stays, and over 4,000 square metres of conference space.

Grosvenor House Hotel

www.grosvenorhouse-dubai.com 04 399 8888

A Le Meridien-owned property, this was the first luxury resort to open in Dubai Marina and every one of its 45 storeys is nothing less than sheer extravagance. For a start, the views are awesome, with the Persian Gulf and bustling Dubai city scenes filling up the landscape. Then there are the butlers on hand to attend to guests staying in any of the 217 chic suites.

Habtoor Grand Resort and Spa

www.habtoorhotels.com 04 399 5000

On the site of the former Metropolitan Resort & Beach Club, the Habtoor Grand Resort and Spa now offers 442 beautifully furnished, spacious rooms and suites with garden or sea views. Pools, restaurants and bars are set amid the hotel's tropical gardens bordering the Arabian Gulf. Food and drink options include Mun Chi for Asian-fusion and British pub, The Underground.

Hilton Dubai Creek

www.hilton.com 04 227 1111

From the lobby to the stairwells, this hotel has been beautifully designed – thanks to the talent of Carlos Ott it feels more like a gallery than a hotel. If the 154 elegant guestrooms aren't enough to have you clambering though the lobby then Verre, Gordon Ramsey's celebrated restaurant, should do the trick. Oddly situated for such a highbrow place, but perhaps that's its charm.

Hilton Dubai Jumeriah

www.hilton.com 04 399 1111

Most of the 389 rooms and suites at this beachfront hotel overlook luxurious gardens and face the sea, which more than compensates for the nearby construction. A good range of watersports are provided at the hotel by Fun Sports, while the hotel attracts many non-guests to its first-class restaurants including BiCE, the highly acclaimed Italian.

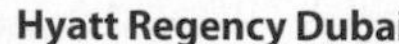

Hyatt Regency Dubai

www.dubai.regency.hyatt.com 04 209 1234

Hyatt Regency's recent refurbishments are breathing new life into what were already some of Dubai's most popular restaurants. Venues such as Miyako (Japanese), Focaccia (Mediterranean) and Shahrzad (Persian) are all excellent, while Al Dawaar, Dubai's only revolving restaurant, offers great views of the creek and coast. All 400 guest rooms and serviced suites have a sea view.

Jebel Ali Golf Resort & Spa

www.jebelalihotel.com 04 883 6000

This is the oldest resort on the block. It opened in 1981, way before the glitz and glamour, so expect less frills but equal, if not better, customer service than newer rivals. Despite its age, the facilities are still well up to par with secluded beaches, landscaped gardens and what was once the region's only golf course. Horse riding and a variety of water sports are also on offer.

Jumeriah Beach Club

www.jumeriahbeachclub.com 04 344 5333

Hidden behind high walls and excessive foliage, The Jumeirah Beach Club screams exclusivity. There are 48 secluded suites (each with their own balcony or garden) and two luxury villas nestled among the club's manicured gardens and private beach. Its signature restaurant, Prasinos, is one of Dubai's finest, serving top-class Mediterranean cuisine, while the Satori Spa is heaven on earth.

Jumeriah Beach Hotel

www.jumeriah.com 04 348 0000

The ocean wave to the Burj's sail, Jumeriah Beach is another famous landmark on the coast. Inspired by the region's seafaring tradition, the nautical theme runs through everything here, from the colourful lobby decor to the stylish interior of the 618 sea-view rooms. Guests and visitors are spoilt for dining choice with 25 restaurants, cafes and bars to choose from.

JW Marriott Hotel

www.marriott-middleeast.com 04 348 0000

Located in the middle of bustling Deira, overlooking the creek, The Marriott boasts 305 rooms and 39 suites. Among its 13 bars and restaurants are the popular Cucina and The Market Place and Champions – one of Dubai's best bars for sports fans. You'll also find the Middle East's largest skylight and, bizarrely, an indoor town square.

Kempinski Hotel

www.kempinski-dubai.com 04 341 0000

Emirates brings one of the world's biggest hotel chains to Dubai. The Kempinski offers a very leisurely experience with its luxury health club, Ayurveda wellness centre and the Middle East's first indoor ski resort, Ski Dubai.The hotel includes ski chalets with breathtaking views over the ski slopes and snow park. And that's before we even get to Apres...

Le Meridien Mina Seyahi

www.lemeridien-minaseyai.com 04 399 3333

The focus here is on water-related fun as the resort takes full advantage of its fabulous 500-metre long private beachfront. The hotel is home to the Offshore Powerboat Championships, as well as other racing competitions and boasts it own world-class marina with over 140 berths. Not to be confused with the nearby Le Royal Meridien.

Metropolitan Palace Hotel

www.habtoorhotels.com 04 227 0000

An elegant lobby, 212 tasteful rooms and a rooftop swimming pool are the main selling points of this hotel, along with its affordable room rate. The convenient location, one block from the creek in Deira, also merits a thumbs up. Tahiti, its Polynesian restaurant, is great for a lively night out, while cosmopolitan Sketch offers creative European cuisine.

Madinat Jumeirah

www.jumeirah.com 04 366 8888

Huge, hugely extravagant and styled after a traditional Arabian citadel, the Madinat (or city in Arabic) is home to two lavish boutique hotels (Al Qasr and Mina A'Salam), courtyard summer houses and the Six Senses Spa, all reached by abra (traditional boat). Between the two hotels lies the hedonistic playground of Souk Madinat, with bars and cafes galore.

Movenpick Hotel Bur Dubai

www.movenpick-hotels.com 04 341 0000

Located near Lamcy Plaza and Wafi City, this hotel offers a high standard of service in keeping with the chain's Swiss heritage. Although you can dine in the impressive lobby, you shouldn't miss the chance to eat at Fakhreldine, one of Dubai's best Lebanese restaurants. And the nightclub downstairs, the well-known Jimmy Dix, is good for guilty pleasures.

One&Only Royal Mirage 04 399 9999

www.oneandonlyroyalmirage.com

This is what most first-time visitors expect of Dubai: traditional Arabesque design, Bedouin beauty and the very best in hospitality. Of all the resorts and hotels in Dubai, this has to be the calmest and most understated. Sundowners here are a must as is a night at signature restaurant, Tagine, or a twirl on the dance floor of its popular nightclub, Kasbar.

Park Hyatt 04 341 0000

www.dubai.park.hyatt.com

Dubai's latest five-star hotel commands a prime waterfront location over the creek next to Dubai Creek Golf & Yacht Club. The hotel is Mediterranean in style with low buildings, natural colours, and stylish decor illuminated by candles at night, and all 225 rooms have a balcony with a great view. The hotel's luxurious spa can provide treatments in your room.

Ritz-Carlton, Dubai

www.ritzcarlton.com 04 399 4000

The rich tradition of The Ritz-Carlton franchise can be felt throughout its hotel in Dubai. Each of its 138 guest rooms comes with its own balcony or patio and spectacular view. And its Splendido and La Baie restaurants are two of the city's finest. White sandy beachfront and stunning views of the Arabian Gulf offset the hotel's spectacular Mediterranean architecture.

Shangri-La Hotel

www.shangri-la.com 04 343 8888

It opened to mixed reviews, but the Shangri-La has since won the hearts of the city and its visitors. Its location on the busy Sheikh Zayed Road makes it an excellent choice for the business traveller, and since its luxuries and indulgences are many – from the opulent lobby to the variety of restaurants and cafes available – every visit is a pleasant experience.

SAS Radisson, Dubai Creek

www.radissonsas.com 04 222 7171

During 2005, the hotel's 30th anniversary year, the old InterCon received a facelift and is now under new management. Its location right on the creekside in Deira means traffic and parking can be a hindrance, but the restaurants, offering seafood, Italian, and Chinese, and its chilled cocktail bar Kubu make the smog worthwhile.

SAS Radisson, Dubai Media City

www.dubai.radissonsas.com 04 366 9111

The location of this brand-new addition to Dubai's hotel scene is hard to beat, especially if you want to mix business with pleasure. Not only is it located in Dubai Media City, it is also close to the upcoming Marsa Dubai area and the beach. The 246 rooms and suites are well equipped, plus there are a number of stylish food and drink outlets fit for nearby media types.

Sheraton Dubai Creek Hotel

www.sheraton.com/dubai 04 228 1111

Like other hotels located in this part of town, the 255-room Sheraton underwent massive renovations in 2002. Its prime location on the bank of the creek means most rooms have beautiful views. Two of its restaurants are also outstanding: Ashiana, regarded as one of the best traditional Indian restaurants in Dubai, and Vivaldi, a wonderful Italian.

Sheraton Jumeirah Beach Resort

www.starwoodhotels.com 04 399 5533

An oldie but a goodie, this hotel is a little further up Jumeirah's beach strip but still close enough for guests to appreciate downtown Dubai. The 255 guestrooms are all delightfully bright and airy and the 12 restaurants in the resort will stop the belly grumbles quick smart. The hotel has good health and sports facilities and is minutes from Emirates Golf club.

Sofitel City Centre Hotel

www.deiracitycentre.com 04 294 1222

Adjoining one of the Middle East's largest and busiest shopping centres, Deira City Centre, this hotel is great if you're in town for retail therapy. Some of the 327 rooms have a good view over the greens of Dubai Creek Golf & Yacht Club and the hotel also features good conference facilities, serviced apartments, four restaurants and a traditional English pub.

Desert resorts

Why limit yourself to one luxurious hotel in the city, when there are a few more tucked away in the desert? One way to sample another five stars is to head out to the dunes for peace and quiet amid one of Dubai's desert resorts. One of the most popular and exclusive is Al Maha Desert Resort & Spa, which is owned and managed by Emirates Airlines. Its chairman Sheikh Ahmed bin Saeed Al Maktoum came up with the idea of this world-renowned 'eco-tourism resort' that in turn spawned the Dubai Desert Conservation Reserve (DDCR), which now encompasses nearly 5% of the emirate.

Al Maha Desert Resort & Spa

www.al-maha.com 04 343 9595

Set within a 225-square-kilometre conservation reserve, this luxury getaway describes itself as 'The World's first Arabian eco-tourism resort'. It resembles a typical Bedouin camp, but conditions at Al Maha are anything but basic. Each suite has its own private pool, and guests can dine on their own veranda. Activities include horse riding, camel trekking and falconry.

Bab Al Shams Desert Resort & Spa

www.jumeriahbabalshams.com 04 832 6699

Bab Al Shams, which translates as 'The Gateway to the Sun', is an elegant desert resort set in a traditional Arabic fort. It's also home to the region's first authentic open air Arabic desert restaurant, Al Hadheerah. There's a kids' club, health and leisure facilities including Satori Spa, and a desert-side swimming pool and bar with breathtaking views over the dunes.

J

K

L

M

N

O

P

Q

R

S

Explorer Products

Residents' Guides

All you need to know about living, working and enjoying...

Activity Guides

Drive, trek, dive and swim... life will never be boring again.

UAE off-road | Oman off-road | Oman trekking | UAE underwater

Mini Guides

The perfect pocket-sized Visitors' Guides.

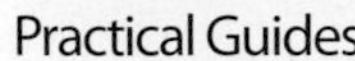

Practical Guides

You've got questions, these books have answers.

Lifestyle Products

The perfect accessories for a buzzing lifestyle.

Map Guides

Wherever you are, never get lost again.

Calendars

The time, the place and the date.

Photography Books

Beautiful cities caught through the lens.

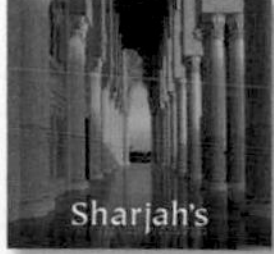

Explorer Team

Publisher
Alistair MacKenzie

Editorial
Managing Editor Claire England
Editors David Quinn, Jane Roberts, Tim Binks, Sean Kearns
Deputy Editors Jeanne Davies, Becky Lucas
Sub Editor Jo Holden-MacDonald
Editorial Assistants Helga Becker, Wenda Oosterbroek, Mariella Stankova

Design
Design Manager Pete Maloney
Senior Designers Ieyad Charaf, Alex Jeffries
Designer Jayde Fernandes
Cartographers Zainudheen Madathil, Noushad Madathil
Design Admin Manager Shyrell Tamayo

Photography
Photography Manager Pamela Grist

Sales & Marketing
Sales Manager Alena Hykes
Sales Executive Laura Zuffa
International Sales Manager Ivan Rodrigues
Business Development Shine Ebrahim
Marketing Executive Marileze Jacobsz-Robson
Merchandisers Abdul Gafoor, Firos Khan, Mannie Lugtu, Ahmed Mainodin

Finance & Administration
Administration Manager Andrea Fust
Accounts Assistant Cherry Enriquez
Administrators Enrico Maullon, **Driver** Rafi Jamal

IT
IT Administrator Ajay Krishnan R.
Senior IT Engineer Smitha Sadanand

Email relevant person at Firstname@Explorer-Publishing.com